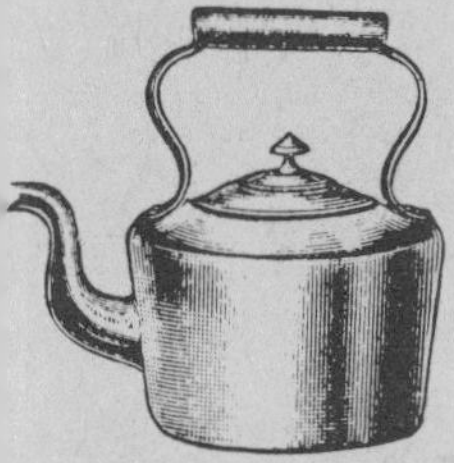

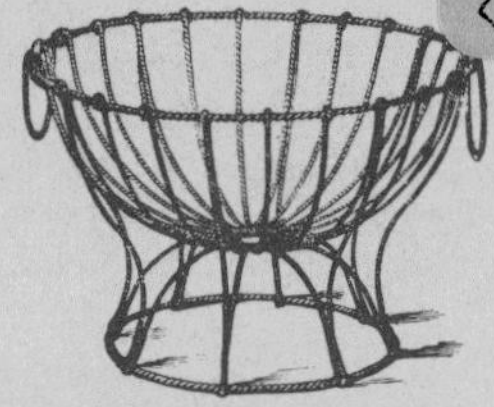

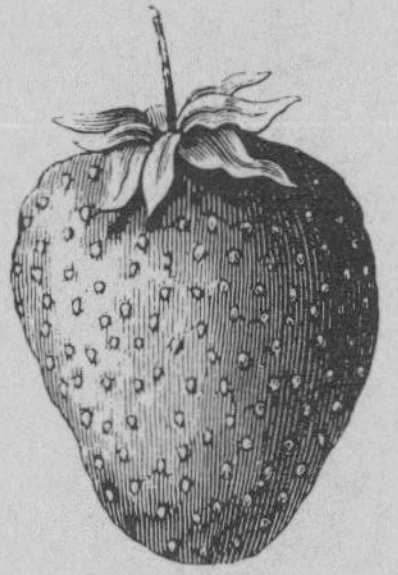

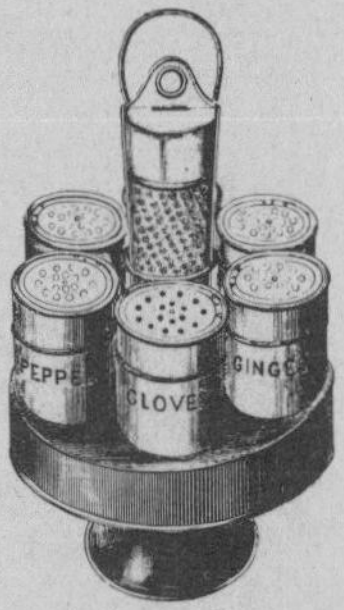
CLOVES

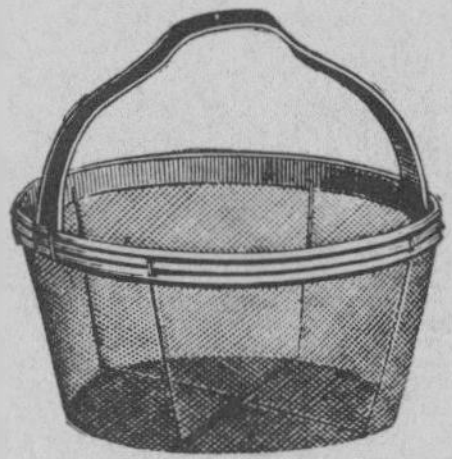

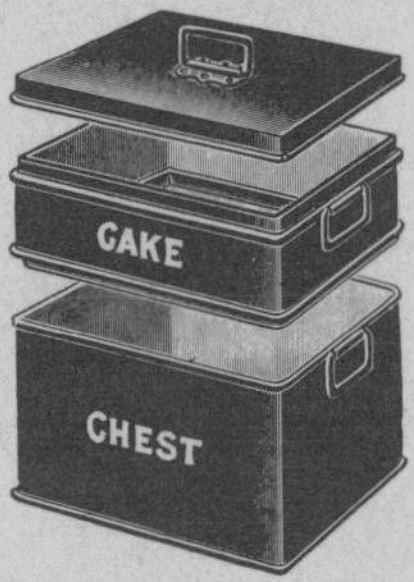
CAKE
CHEST

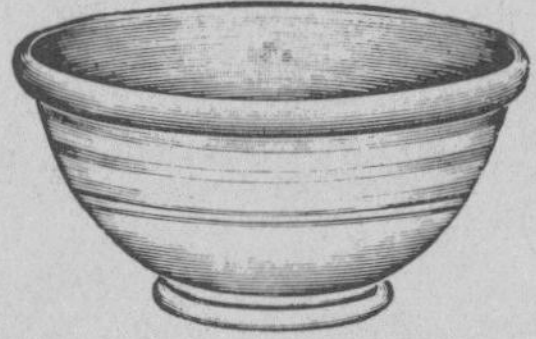

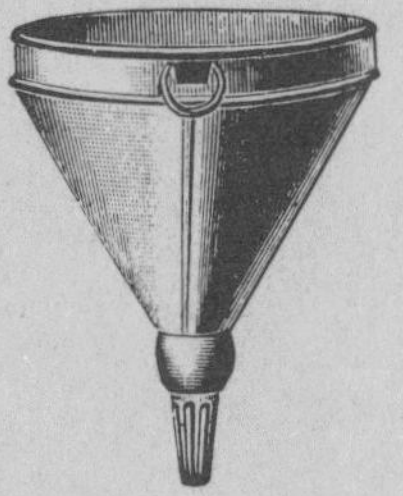

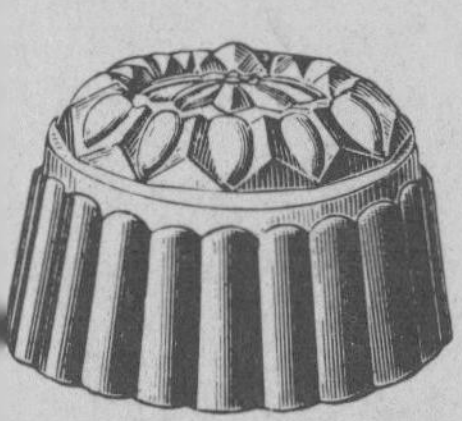

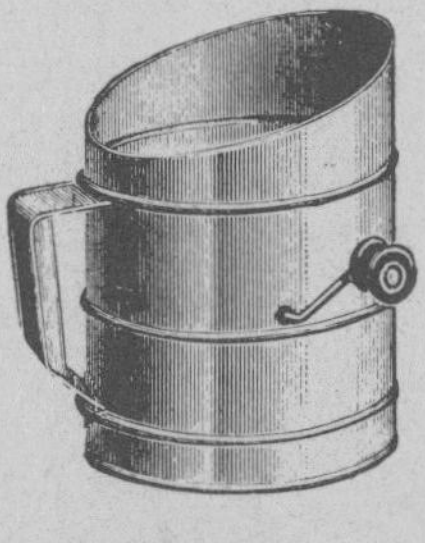

Southern Living.

The
SOUTHERN
HERITAGE
COOKBOOK
LIBRARY

The SOUTHERN HERITAGE
Celebrations
COOKBOOK

OXMOOR HOUSE
Birmingham, Alabama

Southern Living

The Southern Heritage Cookbook Library

The Southern Heritage CELEBRATIONS Cookbook

Manager, Editorial Projects: Ann H. Harvey
Southern Living® *Foods Editor*: Jean W. Liles
Production Editor: Joan E. Denman
Foods Editor: Katherine M. Eakin
Director, Test Kitchen: Laura N. Nestelroad
Test Kitchen Home Economists: Pattie B. Booker, Kay E. Clarke,
   Marilyn L. Hannan, Elizabeth J. Taliaferro
Production Manager: Jerry R. Higdon
Copy Editor: Melinda E. West
Editorial Assistant: Karen P. Traccarella
Food Photographer: Jim Bathie
Food Stylist: Sara Jane Ball
Layout Designer: Christian von Rosenvinge
Mechanical Artist: Faith Nance
Research Assistant: Janice Randall

Special Consultants

Art Director: Irwin Glusker
Heritage Consultant: Meryle Evans
Foods Writer: Lillian B. Marshall
Food and Recipe Consultants: Marilyn Wyrick Ingram,
   Audrey P. Stehle

Cover: The Fourth of July Stars and Stripes menu begins on page 83.
Photograph by George Ratkai.

CONTENTS

INTRODUCTION

rom one New Year's party to the next, the year is hardly long enough for all the seasonally oriented fun, feasting, and foolishness the South engages in. Just name an occasion; Southerners will celebrate it. We may not all observe it in exactly the same manner, but we do believe in making the most of our holidays. So in between the main events in this book, you will find other celebrations that take place only in the South.

Although we open with New Year's, our calendar of holidays actually goes in a circle, not a straight line. New Year's, after all, is but a rowdy stopover between Christmas and Twelfth Night. After a quick bow to St. Valentine, we're ready to take leave of our senses and indulge in a true gale-force pre-Lenten Mardi Gras. Then, without dropping a stitch, everyone puts on green for St. Pat's Day and tries to eat his weight in corned beef and cabbage. That's by way of clearing the palate before the feast days of Easter and Passover set in.

Springtime in the South brings the garden pilgrimages that act as magnets to our friends from the North. And Spring is a giddy time for the natives as well. May Day, like St. Valentine's and Halloween, is party time for children, and for that reason we have included outings geared to youngsters, with fun foods that are familiar enough to be trusted while looking different enough to pique their interest.

On the first Saturday in May, Louisville revels in its unique claim to fame: The Kentucky Derby, most famous horse race in the world. Lavish is the word for parties given by horse people, always has been.

No Southern celebration is more meaningful or more jublilant than Independence Day. . .the Fourth of July. Bands playing, flags flying, it is feast time again. But mostly outdoors, with barbecue grills working full tilt, parks filling wall-to-wall with picnickers, and ice cream freezers cranking out everybody's favorite flavor by the gallon.

Come with us to Thanksgiving dinners on both the eastern and western edges of the South. And fall to, bib and tucker, when Christmas is celebrated in many of its regional manifestations. You're invited. And, if you like knowing what has gone before, there is history woven into the fabric of our Southern celebrations.

Happy New Year!

Since early civilization, through many kinds of time reckoning, man has celebrated his oldest holiday: the year's beginning. In Babylon, New Year's Day was observed as early as 2600 B.C. in a festival for the deity, Marduk, with dramatic productions illustrating his death and rebirth. As in Persia and Russia, the Babylonian New Year coincided with the Spring Equinox. The Egyptians began their year's cycle with the summer flooding of the Nile; American Indians equated the beginning of a new year with the running of salmon and the ripening of acorns.

Romans opened the year with the Festival of Ancyclia in March, and the year consisted of only ten months until Numa Pompilius added January and February. It was Julius Caesar who employed an Egyptian astronomer to revise the calendar in order to bring the religious and solar years into balance. The Julian calendar was in use until Pope Gregory established January 1 as New Year's Day.

Catholics everywhere accepted the Gregorian Calendar in 1582; Scotland followed in 1600. But Protestants in England and America clung to the Julian system, with March 25 as New Year's Day, until September, 1752. There was confusion aplenty. George Washington was born February 12, 1732, "old style," and it was not until around 1800 that his birthday was designated officially as February 22, "new style."

The Chinese observe New Year's between January 21 and February 19. The Jewish New Year may start anywhere between September 6 and October 9.

In the early days of Christianity, New Year's rites were soberly religious, in contrast with the pagan goings-on of non-believers. Hindus had it both ways, first offering sacrifices to the god of wisdom, then moving on to more frivolous activities. English Puritans scorned the "pagan" holiday, an attitude they brought to these shores in the 1600s. The idea of the New Year being represented by a baby is credited to the Germans.

Collection of Business Americana

Wishing You A Happy New Year.

A New Year's greeting card c.1900.

Chilled Champagne, Crabmeat Mold, and Cucumber Ring Canapés.

NEW YEAR'S EVE BUFFET

Just within the past generation or two, the buffet style of dinner service has emerged as the tactic of choice of many party givers. This New Year's Eve menu reflects a part of the evolution in lifestyle that has overtaken the South as much as the rest of the country.

Most of us fete our guests with fairly informal gatherings compared with our grand-mothers' social functions, which sometimes ran to as much starch in the party as in the linens. Although we are less formal today, a well thought-out buffet can still say "How clever" and "How beautiful," because it is all spread out to be seen as one composition instead of being brought on in courses.

Here we send the old year out in the best of spirits...the easy way.

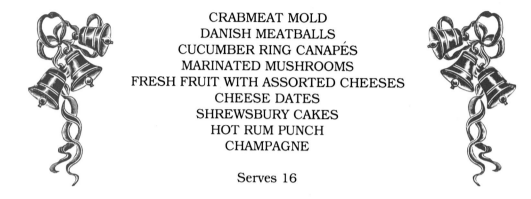

CRABMEAT MOLD
DANISH MEATBALLS
CUCUMBER RING CANAPÉS
MARINATED MUSHROOMS
FRESH FRUIT WITH ASSORTED CHEESES
CHEESE DATES
SHREWSBURY CAKES
HOT RUM PUNCH
CHAMPAGNE

Serves 16

Nineteenth-century card wishes "Joy and peace this glad New Year."

CRABMEAT MOLD

1½ envelopes unflavored
  gelatin
3 tablespoons boiling water
¼ cup lemon juice
1½ cups fresh crabmeat,
  drained and flaked
1¼ cups chopped celery
2 (3-ounce) jars
  pimiento-stuffed olives,
  drained and sliced
2 tablespoons chopped
  pimiento
2 cups mayonnaise
1 to 2 teaspoons hot sauce
½ teaspoon salt
¼ teaspoon pepper
Leaf lettuce
Cooked shrimp
Additional sliced
  pimiento-stuffed olives
Fresh parsley sprigs

Dissolve gelatin in boiling
water; stir in lemon juice. Set
aside to cool.

Combine crabmeat, celery,
olives, and pimiento in a large
bowl; set aside.

Add mayonnaise, hot sauce,
salt, and pepper to dissolved gelatin mixture. Stir well, and fold
into crabmeat mixture.

Spoon mixture into a lightly
oiled 5-cup mold. Refrigerate
until firm. Invert onto a lettuce-
lined platter. Garnish with
shrimp, additional olive slices,
and parsley. Serve with crackers. Yield: 16 servings.

DANISH MEATBALLS

1 pound ground beef
1 medium onion, finely
  chopped
1 egg, beaten
1 cup fine, dry breadcrumbs
1 tablespoon milk
1 teaspoon salt
½ teaspoon pepper
¼ cup vegetable oil
¼ cup all-purpose flour
2 cups water
Salt and pepper to taste

Combine beef, onion, egg,
breadcrumbs, milk, salt, and
pepper, mixing well. Shape mixture into 1-inch meatballs.
Brown in oil in a large skillet
over medium heat. Remove
meatballs from skillet, and
drain on paper towels. Reserve
pan drippings in skillet.

Add flour to pan drippings,
stirring until smooth. Cook 1
minute, stirring constantly.
Gradually add water; cook over
medium heat, stirring constantly, until thickened and
bubbly. Stir in salt and pepper
to taste. Add meatballs to gravy.
Cover and simmer 30 minutes.
Yield: about 16 servings.

CUCUMBER RING
CANAPÉS

3 (3-ounce) packages cream
  cheese, softened
2 tablespoons mayonnaise
3 tablespoons freeze-dried
  chives
1½ tablespoons minced fresh
  parsley
¼ teaspoon paprika
1 large cucumber, peeled and
  cored
1 (8-ounce) loaf sliced party
  rye bread

Combine first 5 ingredients;
mix well. Place mixture in a
pastry bag, and chill.

Cut cucumber into ⅛-inch
slices; drain well.

Place one cucumber ring on
each slice of bread. Pipe cream
cheese mixture into center of
each ring. Chill. Yield: about 2½
dozen.

MARINATED
MUSHROOMS

1½ pounds fresh mushrooms
¼ cup finely chopped celery
2 cloves garlic, minced
¼ cup butter or margarine,
  melted
¼ cup water
1 cup vinegar
1 cup olive oil
¼ cup lemon juice
2 tablespoons chopped fresh
  parsley
2 bay leaves
1 teaspoon coarsely ground
  black pepper
¼ teaspoon dried whole
  oregano

Clean mushrooms with damp
paper towels. Combine mushrooms, celery, garlic, butter,
and water in a large skillet;
bring to a boil. Reduce heat;
cover and simmer 5 minutes.
Add remaining ingredients,
stirring well. Cover and simmer
3 minutes. Let cool. Marinate in
refrigerator several hours or
overnight. Remove mushrooms
from marinade before serving.
Yield: 16 servings.

CHEESE DATES

1½ cups (6 ounces) shredded
   sharp Cheddar cheese
1 cup all-purpose flour
1 teaspoon salt
⅛ to ¼ teaspoon red pepper
¼ cup plus 2 tablespoons
   butter or margarine, melted
28 pitted dates
28 pecan halves
1 egg white
Sifted powdered sugar
   (optional)

Combine cheese, flour, salt, pepper, and butter; mix well. Set aside.

Make a lengthwise slit in each date and stuff with a pecan half. Press about 2 teaspoons cheese mixture around each date, covering completely. Chill at least 30 minutes.

Remove dates from refrigerator, and brush with egg white. Place on lightly greased baking sheets. Bake at 350° for 25 minutes. Remove dates to a wire rack; cool completely. Sprinkle with powdered sugar, if desired. Yield: about 2 dozen.

A HAPPY NEW YEAR

SHREWSBURY CAKES

1 cup butter or margarine,
   softened
1¾ cups sugar, divided
2 eggs
2 tablespoons brandy
3 cups all-purpose flour
½ teaspoon ground nutmeg
¾ cup currants

Cream butter; gradually add 1½ cups sugar, beating well. Add eggs and brandy, beating well. Combine flour and nutmeg; add to creamed mixture, beating well. Stir in currants.

Shape dough into 1½-inch balls; place 4 inches apart on greased baking sheets. Flatten each ball to ¼-inch thickness; sprinkle with remaining sugar. Bake at 375° for 12 minutes or until edges are lightly browned. Yield: 3½ dozen.

HOT RUM PUNCH

4 cups light rum
2 cups Cognac
2 cups Cointreau or other
   orange-flavored liqueur
1 cup sugar
1 orange, thinly sliced
1 lemon, thinly sliced
8 cups boiling water

Combine rum, Cognac, Cointreau, sugar, orange, and lemon in a heat-proof punch bowl. Add boiling water; stir well. Serve hot. Yield: 16 cups.

Photographed at Mordecai House, Raleigh, North Carolina: Hot Rum Punch, Cheddar in antique caddy, Shrewsbury Cakes (center), and Cheese Dates.

HOGMANAY

The long span of days comprising the Christmas holidays has been called "the daft days" in Scotland. December 31, the last day of the year, is called Hogmanay or "Old Year's Night" and may be the most popular of the "daft" days. Tradition had children dressing up in bedsheets to go from house to house singing and calling out "Hogmanay," whereupon the householder would give out small gifts of food or coins. The poorer children also asked for bread and cheese. Then, with their loot concealed in the giant wrinkles of their costumes, the youngsters would be off to the next house.

The Scottish Black Bun is one of the best known specialties of the holiday.

FORFAR BRIDIES
SAUSAGE ROLLS
SHORTBREAD
DUNLOP CHEESE WITH CRACKERS
BLACK BUN
DUNDEE CAKE
HOGMANAY PUNCH

Serves 8 to 10

FORFAR BRIDIES

½ pound ground beef
¼ pound ground pork
½ cup chopped onion
½ tablespoon chopped
   fresh parsley
½ teaspoon salt
¼ teaspoon pepper
1 (17¼-ounce) package
   commercial puff pastry
Melted butter or margarine

Combine beef, pork, and onion in a large skillet; cook until meat is browned, stirring to crumble. Drain well on paper towels. Combine meat mixture, parsley, salt, and pepper, mixing well.

Thaw pastry according to package directions. Cut pastry into 3½-inch circles. Place about 1 tablespoon meat mixture on each pastry circle. Moisten edges of pastry with water; fold in half, making sure edges are even. Using a fork dipped in flour, press edges of pastry together to seal.

Place on baking sheet and bake at 375° for 20 minutes or until pastry is golden brown. Brush with melted butter. Yield: about 1 dozen.

SAUSAGE ROLLS

1 (12-ounce) package link
   sausage
1 (17¼-ounce) package
   commercial puff pastry

Cook sausage in a large heavy skillet until browned; drain well, and set aside.

Thaw pastry according to package directions. Cut pastry into 3- x 4-inch rectangles; place 1 sausage link lengthwise down center of each pastry rectangle. Roll up jellyroll fashion, pinching edges to seal. Place sausage rolls, seam side down, on a lightly greased baking sheet. Bake at 350° for 25 minutes or until pastry is golden brown. Yield: 1 dozen.

SHORTBREAD

1 cup butter, softened
½ cup sugar
2 cups all-purpose
   flour

Cream butter; gradually add sugar and flour to make a stiff dough. Press mixture into a greased 9-inch tart pan or shortbread mold. Bake at 325° for 40 minutes or until lightly browned. Remove from pan; cool on wire rack. Cut into wedges. Yield: 8 to 10 servings.

The old Scottish custom of "first footing" has a charming ring today. According to Scottish superstition, the first guests of the New Year to cross the thresholds of their friends were the most important. It was good fortune for the household if a dark-haired man came first; bad luck would follow if the first footer happened to be deformed in any way, or red-haired, or a woman.

BLACK BUN

4 cups all-purpose flour,
  divided
½ teaspoon baking powder
½ cup butter or margarine,
  softened
¼ cup plus 2 tablespoons
  cold water
1 (15-ounce) package raisins
1 (10-ounce) package currants
3 (2½-ounce) packages
  blanched almonds, chopped
1 cup sugar
1 teaspoon cream of tartar
1 teaspoon baking powder
2 teaspoons ground allspice
1 teaspoon ground cinnamon
1 teaspoon ground ginger
¼ teaspoon pepper
1 cup milk
1 tablespoon brandy
1 egg, beaten

Combine 2 cups flour and baking powder in a medium mixing bowl. Cut in butter with a pastry blender until mixture resembles coarse meal. Sprinkle cold water evenly over surface; stir with a fork until dry ingredients are moistened. Shape into a ball; chill.

Divide dough into 3 portions. Combine 2 portions of pastry and roll to ⅛-inch thickness on a lightly floured board; fit into a greased 9- x 5- x 3-inch loafpan.

Combine raisins, currants, and almonds in a large mixing bowl; stir well. Combine remaining 2 cups flour, sugar, cream of tartar, baking powder, spices, and pepper; mix well. Add to raisin mixture, stirring well. Add milk and brandy; stirring well. Spoon filling into prepared pastry-lined loafpan.

Roll remaining pastry to ⅛-inch thickness; carefully place over filling, leaving a 1-inch overhang around edge of loafpan. Seal edges and flute; cut slits in top. Brush with egg.

Bake at 225° for 3 hours or until lightly browned. Cool in pan 15 minutes. Remove from pan; place on a wire rack, and let cool completely. Yield: 1 loaf.

Hogmanay pipers, Carlyle House, Alexandria, Virginia.

Traditional Scottish Hogmanay Punch and Dundee Cake.

DUNDEE CAKE

1 cup golden raisins
1 cup raisins
1 cup currants
¾ cup candied red cherries,
  chopped
½ cup candied mixed fruit,
  finely chopped
1 cup ground almonds
2 cups butter or margarine,
  softened
2 cups sugar
Grated rind of 2 lemons
6 eggs
4½ cups all-purpose flour
2 tablespoons baking powder
2 tablespoons sherry
3 tablespoons blanched
  almonds

Combine raisins, currants, cherries, mixed fruit, and ground almonds; set aside.

Cream butter in a large mixing bowl; gradually add sugar and lemon rind, beating until light and fluffy. Add eggs, one at a time, beating well after each addition.

Sift together flour and baking powder; add to creamed mixture, mixing well. Stir in sherry and fruit mixture; mix well.

Spoon batter into a waxed paper-lined and greased 10-inch tube pan. Arrange blanched almonds on top of batter. Bake at 325° for 1 hour. Cover pan with foil, and bake an additional hour or until a wooden pick inserted in center comes out clean. Let cool 20 minutes in pan. Remove cake from pan; place on wire rack and cool completely. Yield: one 10-inch cake.

HOGMANAY PUNCH

Ice cubes
1 (12-ounce) bottle ale,
  preferrably Scottish
¾ cup Scotch whiskey
¾ cup apple cider

Place ice cubes in a chilled punch bowl. Add ale, Scotch, and cider. Stir well; serve over ice cubes. Yield: 3 cups.

GOOD LUCK TO YOU!

As any Southerner knows, it can be downright dangerous not to eat black-eyed peas or Hoppin' John on New Year's Day to ensure good luck for the coming year. Documentation is scarce, but many runs of bad luck have been traced to such a lapse in judgment.

In every culture, foods and feasting have been associated with luck. In Germany, it was once thought wise to eat as richly as possible on New Year's and to dress up as well, just to get into the posture of someone upon whom good luck is about to rain. The French eat pancakes to attract luck, the Ceylonese, rice cakes. Here are some other extremely lucky dishes.

BLOODY MARYS
OVEN-BARBECUED COUNTRY PORK RIBS
BLACK-EYED PEAS WITH HAM HOCK
HOPPING JOHN
FRESH TURNIP GREENS
KENTUCKY CORNBREAD
CREAM CHEESE POUND CAKE * SUGAR CRISPS
HOT RUM TEA

Serves 8

BLOODY MARYS

6 cups spicy tomato cocktail
¼ cup plus 2 tablespoons lemon juice
1¼ teaspoons hot sauce
1 teaspoon Worcestershire sauce
2 teaspoons sugar
1 teaspoon coarsely ground black pepper
½ teaspoon salt
1½ cups vodka
Ice cubes

Combine first 7 ingredients, mixing well. Stir in vodka, and pour over ice cubes to serve. Yield: about 8 cups.

OVEN-BARBECUED COUNTRY PORK RIBS

¼ cup vegetable oil, divided
1 small onion, finely chopped
1 clove garlic, minced
1 (6-ounce) can tomato paste
¾ cup water
½ cup vinegar
2 tablespoons sugar
4 whole cloves
1 tablespoon Worcestershire sauce
1 bay leaf
1½ teaspoons salt
1 teaspoon dry mustard
⅛ teaspoon pepper
⅛ teaspoon chili powder
4 drops hot sauce
4 to 5 pounds pork ribs

Sauté onion and garlic in 1 tablespoon oil over medium heat until golden brown. Add remaining ingredients, except ribs; bring to a boil. Reduce heat; cover and simmer sauce 45 minutes.

Place ribs in a single layer in a 13- x 9- x 2-inch baking pan; brush with remaining oil. Bake at 325° for 40 minutes. Drain off pan drippings, and discard. Pour barbecue sauce over ribs. Bake at 325° 40 minutes or until ribs are tender. Remove cloves and bay leaf before serving. Yield: 8 servings.

HOPPING JOHN

6 slices bacon, diced
1 onion, whole
6 cups water
1 cup dried black-eyed
  peas
1 cup regular rice
1 teaspoon salt
½ teaspoon pepper

Combine bacon, onion, and water in a large Dutch oven. Bring to a boil; cover and simmer 20 minutes. Add peas; cover and simmer 1 hour and 45 minutes or until peas are tender.

Remove onion; discard. Stir in rice, salt, and pepper; cover and simmer 20 minutes or until rice is tender. Yield: 8 servings.

FRESH TURNIP GREENS

1 large bunch (about 5
  pounds) turnip greens
⅓ pound salt pork, washed
  and diced
1 cup water
½ cup coarsely chopped
  onion
1 teaspoon sugar
½ teaspoon salt
½ teaspoon pepper

Cut off and discard tough stems and discolored leaves from greens. Wash greens thoroughly and drain.

Cook salt pork in a large Dutch oven over medium heat, stirring frequently, until crisp and brown.

Add water, onion, sugar, salt, pepper, and greens; bring to a boil. Reduce heat and simmer, uncovered, for 2 minutes. Cover and simmer 45 minutes or until tender. Yield: 8 servings.

Oven-Barbecued Country Pork Ribs, Kentucky Cornbread, Hopping John. Hot Rum Tea, Bloody Marys.

BLACK-EYED PEAS WITH HAM HOCK

1 (16-ounce) package dried
  black-eyed peas
10 to 12 cups water, divided
1 (½-pound) ham hock
1 large onion, whole
Salt to taste

Sort and wash peas; place in a large Dutch oven. Cover with water 2 inches above peas (about 5 to 6 cups); let soak overnight. Drain peas; cover with remaining water.

Wash ham hock. Add ham hock and onion to peas, stirring gently. Simmer, allowing some steam to escape, 1 hour or until peas are tender. Remove onion; discard. Remove ham hock; remove meat from bone. Dice meat; stir into peas. Add salt to taste. Yield: 8 to 10 servings.

Festive Greetings, c.1900.

Collection of Business Americana

KENTUCKY CORNBREAD

1½ cups cornmeal
½ cup all-purpose flour
¼ cup sugar
1 tablespoon baking
  powder
1 teaspoon salt
1½ cups milk
2 tablespoons shortening,
  melted

Combine cornmeal, flour, sugar, baking powder, and salt. Stir in milk and shortening, mixing well.

Pour batter into a greased 8-inch square baking pan. Bake at 400° for 30 minutes or until golden brown. Yield: 8 servings.

CREAM CHEESE POUND CAKE

1½ cups butter, softened
1 (8-ounce) package cream
  cheese, softened
3 cups sugar
6 eggs
3 cups sifted cake flour
1 teaspoon vanilla
  extract
½ teaspoon almond
  extract

Cream butter and cream cheese. Gradually add sugar, beating at medium speed of electric mixer 5 minutes or until light and fluffy. Add eggs, one at a time, beating well after each addition. Add flour, stirring until thoroughly combined. Stir in flavorings.

Pour batter into a greased and floured 10-inch tube pan. Bake at 325° for 1½ hours or until a wooden pick inserted in center comes out clean. Cool in pan 10 minutes; remove from pan, and cool completely on wire rack. Yield: one 10-inch cake.

HOT RUM TEA

10 cooking apples, peeled
6 lemons
8 cups water
1½ cups sugar
10 cup-size tea bags
¾ cup dark rum
Apple slices
Lemon slices
Freshly grated nutmeg
  (optional)

Place apples in a large Dutch oven. Peel and juice lemons; add lemon peel and juice to apples. Stir in water and sugar; bring to a boil. Reduce heat; cover and simmer 20 minutes.

Add tea bags; cover and steep 5 minutes. Remove tea bags, apples, and lemon peel; discard. Stir in rum.

Place fresh apple and lemon slices in mugs; pour tea mixture over fruit. Sprinkle with nutmeg, if desired. Serve hot. Yield: about 8 cups.

SUGAR CRISPS

½ cup butter, softened
½ cup sugar
1 egg
½ teaspoon vanilla extract
2 cups all-purpose flour
2 teaspoons baking powder
¼ teaspoon salt
Red and green decorator
  sugar crystals

Cream butter; gradually add sugar, beating well. Add egg and vanilla; mix well.

Sift together flour, baking powder, and salt; gradually add to creamed mixture, beating well after each addition.

Divide dough in half; wrap in waxed paper, and chill at least 2 hours. Roll half of dough to ¼-inch thickness on a lightly floured surface; keep remaining dough chilled. Cut dough with a bell-shaped cookie cutter. Place on greased baking sheets; sprinkle with decorator sugar crystals.

Bake at 350° for 10 minutes or until edges are lightly browned. Cool on a wire rack. Repeat procedure with remaining dough. Yield: about 3½ dozen.

Noisemaking is an integral part of the New Year's celebration because it was originally thought necessary to frighten out the old year to make room for the new. Drums are good, and bells. Some Southerners, as did their great-grandfathers before them, enjoy firing guns to punctuate the occasion.

Some home entertaining at New Year's has given way to celebrations in public and private clubs. To many Southern hosts this is a pernicious development. For those who prefer to party at home a "Good Luck to You" party is quite appropriate.

VISITING DAY

The custom of visiting on New Year's Day flourished from the 1840s through the turn of the century. Men visited; hostesses received. By eleven in the morning, a lady expecting visitors had seeded her card tray with a few of last year's calling cards, lest the first guest be embarrassed at being early. With cake and eggnog on the sideboard, she readied some strengthening whiskey and brandy straights for those men who thought one more eggnog might prove fatal.

In New Orleans, Visiting Day at the turn of the century was a cue for the gentleman to send a "cornet," a cone-shaped paper container filled with little gifts, to his lady. Then, in polished black top hat, he was ready to make rounds.

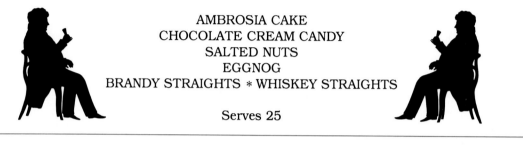

AMBROSIA CAKE
CHOCOLATE CREAM CANDY
SALTED NUTS
EGGNOG
BRANDY STRAIGHTS * WHISKEY STRAIGHTS

Serves 25

Waiting For Calls on New Year's Day, *by Winslow Homer*, Harper's Bazaar, *1869*.

AMBROSIA CAKE

½ cup shortening
2 cups sugar
3 eggs, beaten
2 teaspoons baking soda
1 cup buttermilk
½ cup cocoa
1 cup boiling water
3 cups all-purpose flour
1 teaspoon ground cinnamon
½ teaspoon ground nutmeg
¼ teaspoon ground cloves
1 medium apple, peeled and
  finely chopped
Filling (recipe follows)
Frosting (recipe follows)
Marzipan

Cream shortening and sugar in a large mixing bowl; beat well. Add eggs, mixing well; set aside.

Dissolve soda in buttermilk; set aside. Dissolve cocoa in boiling water, stirring until well blended; set aside.

Combine flour and spices; add to creamed mixture alternately with buttermilk and cocoa mixtures, beginning and ending with flour mixture. Stir in apple.

Pour batter into 4 greased and floured 9-inch round cakepans. Bake at 350° for 20 minutes or until a wooden pick inserted in center comes out clean. Cool in pans 10 minutes; remove from pans, and cool completely.

Spread filling between layers;

spread top and sides of cake with frosting. Garnish top of cake with Marzipan fruit. Yield: one 4-layer cake.

Filling:

1 orange
1 cup whipping cream
4 egg yolks
1 cup sugar
3 tablespoons butter or
  margarine
1½ cups flaked coconut
1 cup currants
1 cup chopped pecans

Grate orange rind; set aside. Remove seeds from orange. Grind orange; set aside.

Combine cream, egg yolks, and sugar in a saucepan; cook over medium heat, stirring constantly, until thickened. Remove from heat; stir in butter.

Stir in orange rind and pulp. Add coconut, currants, and pecans, mixing well. Let cool completely. Yield: enough for one 4-layer cake.

Frosting:

1 tablespoon instant coffee
  granules
⅓ cup boiling water
3 (1-ounce) squares
  unsweetened chocolate
¼ cup butter or margarine
Dash of salt
4 cups sifted powdered sugar

Combine coffee granules and boiling water, stirring until dissolved; set aside.

Combine chocolate, butter, and salt in top of a double boiler. Cook over medium heat, stirring until smooth. Remove from heat; cool.

Stir in coffee mixture. Gradually add powdered sugar, beating at medium speed of electric mixer 1 minute or until mixture is smooth and creamy. Use immediately. Yield: enough for one 4-layer cake.

Marzipan:

½ cup sugar
¼ cup water
1 cup blanched almonds,
  divided
⅛ teaspoon almond extract
1 egg white
2 cups sifted powdered sugar
Assorted food colorings

Position knife blade in processor bowl; add sugar, water, and ½ cup almonds, and cover. Process 30 seconds or until mixture forms a paste. Add remaining almonds and process 1 minute or until mixture is smooth. With processor running, pour almond flavoring through food chute; process 10 seconds or until well mixed.

Place egg whites (at room temperature) in a medium mixing bowl; beat until frothy. Gradually add powdered sugar, beating well to form a soft paste.

Combine egg white mixture and almond mixture, mixing well to form a stiff dough. Refrigerate overnight.

Shape marzipan into assorted miniature fruits and vegetables. Paint with food coloring. Yield: 3 cups.

SALTED NUTS

¾ cup butter, melted
4 cups pecan halves
2 cups whole blanched
  almonds
1 tablespoon salt

Combine butter, pecans, almonds, and salt in a 13- x 9- x 2-inch baking pan. Bake at 350° for 25 minutes, stirring after 15 minutes. Drain on paper towels. Yield: 6 cups.

EGGNOG

2 dozen eggs, separated
2 cups sugar
2 cups milk
2 cups bourbon
1 quart whipping cream,
  whipped
Ground nutmeg

Beat egg yolks in a large bowl until thick and lemon colored. Gradually add sugar, beating constantly. Stir in milk and bourbon, blending well.

Beat egg whites (at room temperature) until stiff. Gently fold egg whites into milk mixture, blending well. Fold in whipped cream. Sprinkle eggnog with nutmeg before serving. Yield: 1½ gallons.

Ambrosia Cake, Eggnog, Chocolate Cream Candy, and Salted Nuts: A sideboard worth visiting.

CHOCOLATE CREAM CANDY

½ cup plus 2 tablespoons
  butter or margarine,
  softened
3½ cups sifted powdered
  sugar
⅛ teaspoon salt
1½ teaspoons vanilla
  extract
6 (1-ounce) squares
  unsweetened chocolate

Cream butter; gradually add sugar and salt, beating until light and fluffy. Add vanilla; blend well.

Shape dough into ¾-inch balls. Place on waxed paper-lined baking sheets.

Place chocolate in top of a double boiler; place over hot water, stirring until chocolate is melted.

Using 2 forks, quickly dip balls, one at a time, into chocolate mixture; return to waxed paper-lined baking sheet. Chill on baking sheets until chocolate is firm. Store in airtight containers in a cool place. Yield: about 3½ dozen.

Eggnog is a cousin, not far removed, of the colonial favorite, syllabub. An old rule of thumb for eggnog was one part brandy or spirits to three parts milk; a dozen eggs to two quarts. President Harrison, "Old Tippecanoe," who won the Presidency as a war hero with a log cabin and a jug of hard cider as symbols, loved eggnog and made it by his own recipe. After all, he was a Virginian; his father, Benjamin, had been governor and had signed the Declaration of Independence.

Twelfth Night

C ounting Christmas as the first night, the twelfth night falls on January 5, the vigil or eve of Epiphany. Twelfth Night is a festival older and technically more important than Christmas itself in parts of Christendom. Epiphany commemorates three crucial events in Christian history: The baptism of Jesus, the visit of the Three Wise Men to Bethlehem, and the Miracle at Cana. It is one of the chief occasions celebrated in England, with feasting and masked balls, and it is a day of gift-giving in many lands.

The custom of choosing a King for Twelfth Night was brought to England by the Romans. The enormous cake baked for Epiphany contained a bean and a pea. When the slices were served, early in the evening, the man who found the bean in his portion was crowned King of the Bean; the pea finder became his queen for the revel.

Twelfth Night revels continued unabated when the colonists brought their time-honored holiday to this country. In old Virginia, Twelfth Night was called Old Christmas and was the occasion of the grandest balls and parties of the year.

Closed, the card becomes bean-shaped!

SOUTH CAROLINA REVEL

The "social board" of the English settlers was seldom so overtaxed with food as it was on Twelfth Night. The Twelfth Night Cake commanded the center of the main table or, if needed, a separate dessert table. Around the great cake were placed trays of tempting little cakes, tarts, nuts, candies, and possibly some sweet treats left from the Christmas holiday baking. Crystal, silver, everything the householder owned, was placed for best effect, and there were so many different dishes that there was scarcely an inch of table showing between them.

OVERNIGHT SMOKED TURKEY
PICKLED SHRIMP
SCALLOPED OYSTERS
MINIATURE ROLLS
SAUTÉED WALNUTS
SUGARED NUTS
TINY SWEET ROLLS
BANBURY TARTS
HOMEMADE FUDGE
CANDIED ORANGE AND LEMON PEEL
TWELFTH NIGHT CAKE
WASSAIL
SHRUB

Serves 12

OVERNIGHT SMOKED TURKEY

1 (12- to 14-pound) turkey
¼ cup vegetable oil
½ cup salt
¼ cup pepper
1 cup vinegar

Remove giblets and neck from turkey; reserve for other uses. Rinse turkey thoroughly with cold water; pat dry. Rub oil over surface of turkey. Combine salt and pepper; sprinkle over surface and in cavity of turkey.

Close cavity of turkey with skewers. Tie ends of tail with string or tuck them under band of skin at tail. Lift wingtips up and over back, tucking under bird securely. Set aside.

Prepare charcoal fire in smoker, and let burn 10 to 15 minutes. Place water pan in smoker, and fill with vinegar. Add enough hot water to fill pan, if necessary.

Place turkey on food rack. Cover with smoker lid; cook about 16 hours, refilling water pan with water, if needed. Turkey is done when drumsticks move easily.

Transfer turkey to a serving platter. Let stand at least 15 minutes before carving. Yield: about 24 servings.

Note: Leftover turkey may be stored for later uses.

PICKLED SHRIMP

5 pounds medium shrimp, peeled, deveined, and cooked
2 medium onions, thinly sliced
3 cups vegetable oil
2 cups vinegar
3 teaspoons celery seeds
2 tablespoons capers, undrained
8 bay leaves
6 drops hot sauce
Lettuce leaves

Place shrimp and onion in a large mixing bowl.

Combine oil, vinegar, celery seeds, capers, bay leaves, and hot sauce in a jar. Cover jar tightly, and shake vigorously. Pour marinade over shrimp and onion mixture; toss well. Cover and refrigerate overnight.

Remove bay leaves; discard. Toss mixture well before serving. Yield: 12 servings.

Twelfth Night Cake
and icy pink Shrub top
off a party meal of
Smoked Turkey, Pickled
Shrimp, Banbury Tarts,
Candied Citrus,
and Miniature Rolls.

SCALLOPED OYSTERS

2 cups finely chopped celery
1¼ cups butter or margarine,
  divided
¼ cup Worcestershire sauce
½ teaspoon salt
½ teaspoon pepper
⅛ teaspoon hot sauce
3 cups cracker crumbs,
  divided
6 (12-ounce) containers fresh
  Select oysters, drained
Paprika

Sauté celery in 1 cup butter
until tender but not brown; stir
in next 4 ingredients.

Place 1 cup cracker crumbs in
bottom of a greased 2-quart casserole. Top with half of oysters
and half of celery mixture. Repeat layers, beginning and ending with cracker crumbs. Melt
remaining butter, and pour over
cracker crumbs. Sprinkle with
paprika. Bake at 350° for 45
minutes or until bubbly. Yield:
12 servings.

MINIATURE ROLLS

1⅓ cups all-purpose flour
⅓ cup sugar
2 teaspoons baking powder
½ teaspoon salt
½ cup milk
2 eggs, beaten
¼ cup butter or margarine,
  melted
Melted butter or margarine

Sift flour, sugar, baking powder, and salt together into a
large mixing bowl. Combine
milk and eggs; add to flour mixture, and stir well. Stir in ¼ cup
melted butter.

Spoon batter into well-
greased miniature muffin pans,
filling two-thirds full. Bake at
400° for 15 minutes or until
golden brown. Brush tops with
melted butter. Yield: 2 dozen.

SAUTÉED WALNUTS

6 cups walnut halves
¾ cup olive oil
1½ tablespoons
  Worcestershire sauce
1½ teaspoons soy sauce
¾ teaspoon salt

Sauté walnuts in oil in a large
skillet 3 minutes or until lightly
browned. Remove from heat,
and add Worcestershire and soy
sauces; mix well. Let stand 5
minutes. Drain walnuts on
paper towels. Sprinkle with salt.
Yield: 6 cups.

SUGARED NUTS

2 cups sugar
½ cup water
1 teaspoon ground cinnamon
⅛ teaspoon cream of tartar
2 teaspoons vanilla extract
4 cups pecan halves

Combine sugar, water, cinnamon, and cream of tartar in a small Dutch oven; stir well. Cook over medium-high heat, stirring constantly until mixture reaches soft ball stage (240°). Remove from heat. Add vanilla and pecans, and stir until sugar begins to harden.

Immediately spread pecans on waxed paper, and separate into clusters with a spoon. Let cool. Yield: about 4 cups.

TINY SWEET ROLLS

Pastry for 9-inch pie
1 tablespoon butter or
  margarine, melted
⅓ cup plus 2 tablespoons
  sugar
1 teaspoon ground cinnamon

Roll pastry to a 12- x 6-inch rectangle, and spread with butter. Combine sugar and cinnamon; sprinkle mixture over rectangle. Roll up jellyroll fashion, beginning at long side; moisten edges with water to seal. Cut into ½-inch slices; place slices, cut side down, in a greased 8-inch round cakepan.

Bake at 400° for 12 minutes or until pastry is flaky and lightly browned. Serve warm. Yield: about 2 dozen.

BANBURY TARTS

1 cup raisins, chopped
¾ cup sugar
1 egg, slightly beaten
1 tablespoon graham cracker
  crumbs
2 teaspoons grated lemon
  rind
1 tablespoon lemon juice
Double-Crust Pastry

Combine first 6 ingredients; mix well, and set aside.

Roll pastry to ⅛-inch thickness on a lightly floured surface; cut into 3-inch squares. Place 2 teaspoons raisin mixture in center of each square. Moisten edges of pastry with water, and fold in half diagonally. Press edges with a fork to seal.

Place tarts on ungreased baking sheets, and bake at 350° for 25 minutes or until lightly browned. Yield: 2 dozen.

Double-Crust Pastry:

2 cups all-purpose flour
½ teaspoon salt
⅔ cup shortening
5 to 6 tablespoons cold water

Combine flour and salt; cut in shortening with a pastry blender until mixture resembles coarse meal. Sprinkle cold water evenly over surface; stir with a fork until dry ingredients are moistened. Shape dough into a ball; chill. Yield: enough pastry for 2 dozen tarts.

HOMEMADE FUDGE

2½ cups sugar
⅔ cup milk
2 (1-ounce) squares
  semi-sweet chocolate
2 tablespoons light corn
  syrup
Dash of salt
2 tablespoons butter
1 teaspoon vanilla
  extract
1 cup chopped pecans

Combine sugar, milk, chocolate, syrup, and salt in a Dutch oven. Cook over low heat, stirring constantly, until sugar is dissolved.

Continue to cook, stirring constantly, until mixture reaches soft ball stage (240°). Remove from heat; add butter and vanilla (do not stir). Cool to lukewarm (110°).

Add pecans; beat with a wooden spoon 2 to 3 minutes or until mixture is thick and begins to lose its gloss. Pour into a buttered 8-inch square pan. Mark warm fudge in 1⅓-inch squares. Cool and cut. Yield: 3 dozen.

CANDIED ORANGE
AND LEMON PEEL

Peel of 6 lemons, cut into
  ¼-inch wide strips
Peel of 4 oranges, cut into
  ¼-inch wide strips
2 cups sugar
1 cup water
Sugar

Place lemon and orange peel in water to cover in a large saucepan; bring to a boil. Boil 20 minutes; drain. Set aside.

Combine 2 cups sugar and water in a medium saucepan; bring to a boil. Cook until mixture reaches thread stage (230°). Add peel; reduce heat, and simmer 5 minutes, stirring frequently. Drain well.

Roll peel, a few pieces at a time, in sugar. Arrange in a single layer on wire racks; let dry several hours. Store in an airtight container. Yield: 3 cups.

Revellers of 1884 gather for the ceremonial cutting of the Twelfth Night Cake.

WASSAIL

2 quarts apple cider
2 cups ginger ale
1 tablespoon honey
3 whole cloves
2 (2-inch) sticks cinnamon
1 medium orange, sliced
1 medium lemon, sliced

Combine ingredients in a Dutch oven; bring to a boil. Reduce heat; simmer 1 hour. Strain mixture, discarding spices. Yield: 10 cups.

SHRUB

1½ quarts cranberry juice cocktail, chilled
1½ quarts ginger ale, chilled
2 cups fresh raspberries
1 pint raspberry sherbet

Combine first 3 ingredients in a punch bowl. Drop sherbet by scoops into punch. Serve immediately. Yield: about 1 gallon.

TWELFTH NIGHT CAKE

1 cup raisins
1 cup currants
1 cup chopped candied pineapple
½ cup chopped candied red cherries
¾ cup bourbon
1½ cups butter or margarine, softened
1½ cups sugar
6 eggs
3 cups all-purpose flour
1 teaspoon ground cinnamon
1 teaspoon ground ginger
½ teaspoon ground nutmeg
1 cup ground almonds
1 dried pinto bean
1 dried black-eyed pea

Combine first 5 ingredients; stir well. Cover mixture; let stand overnight.

Cream butter in a large mixing bowl; gradually add sugar, beating until light and fluffy. Add eggs, one at a time, beating well after each addition.

Sift flour and spices together; gradually add to creamed mixture, mixing well. Stir in almond-fruit mixture.

Spoon batter into a greased and waxed paper-lined 9-inch springform pan. Press bean and pea just below surface of batter.

Bake at 300° for 2 hours or until a wooden pick inserted in center comes out clean. Cool cake completely in pan. Yield: one 9-inch cake.

The East Coast colonials called it "Twelfth Cake." It began with two pounds each of butter and sugar; then eighteen eggs were added, and it went on until the batter was complete with bean and pea. The Twelfth Night Cake has now mercifully settled into a more manageable affair, more like a pound cake and not so highly flavored with ginger and other spices. However, you will still want to bake the bean and the pea into the cake, and cut it early in order to have monarchs on duty.

St. Valentine's Day

We know which day belongs to St. Valentine, but we may not know which St. Valentine we're celebrating. Old official texts list seven Valentines whose feast days occurred on February 14, not including the "veneration," on the same day, "of the head of the eighth."

The St. Valentine popularly believed to be the true patron saint of lovers and help of those unhappy in love was a young Roman priest in the days of the Emperor Claudius. Finding it difficult to induce married men into the military, Claudius passed a law against marriage. Valentine performed marriages in secret, was caught, and executed (beheaded) on February 14, 269 (or 270) A.D.

The new Christian holiday evolved, especially in England, into a time for exchanging love messages and tokens. Samuel Pepys commented in his diary on Valentine's Day, 1667, that his wife had had a fine ring made for him. While the wealthy gave jewels, for others a simple bouquet sufficed to convey the love message. Parties and elaborate balls were given; lovers reveled in their Saint's Day.

The first commercial valentines came out around 1800. Esther Howland of Massachusetts was making valentines of imported laces and fine papers around 1830, a business said to have made for her $100,000 per year.

*An affair of
the heart,
c.1900, signed
"From Winifred."*

LITTLE FOLKS' VALENTINE PARTY

T he key to a successful child's Valentine party is, in a word, simplicity. Stick to the familiar.

A 1937 New Orleans *Times-Picayune* story told of a mother who sent invitations to her daughter's old-fashioned Valentine party in care of the guests' mothers. She included the menu to reassure the mothers that there would be no tummy aches.

To keep young hands busy, the hostess pulled together old hats, aprons, lace curtains, scarves, dresses, and anything that "could be entrusted to the doubtful care of little girls." With safety pins, mirrors, ribbons, and make-up in hand, the girls transformed themselves into Spanish dancers, Victorian ladies, brides, even clowns. Since it was an "old-fashioned" party, a menu similar to ours was served "box-supper style" in heart-shaped boxes tied with ribbon.

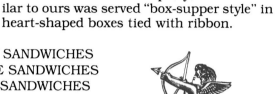

PINWHEEL JELLY SANDWICHES
PIMIENTO CHEESE SANDWICHES
CHICKEN SALAD SANDWICHES
VALENTINE SUGAR COOKIES
HOT CHOCOLATE

Serves 8

PINWHEEL JELLY SANDWICHES

8 slices white bread, crust removed
½ cup creamy peanut butter
About 5 tablespoons strawberry jelly

Using a rolling pin, flatten each slice of bread.

Spread each slice of bread with 1 tablespoon peanut butter and 2 teaspoons strawberry jelly, covering to edges. Roll up bread slices, jellyroll fashion, and wrap each sandwich tightly in waxed paper. Refrigerate overnight.

Remove sandwiches from waxed paper, and cut each sandwich crosswise into four 1-inch pinwheels. Yield: about 3 dozen.

Pimiento Cheese Sandwiches, Pinwheel Sandwiches, Valentine Sugar Cookies, and Hot Chocolate, all little folks' fun food.

PIMIENTO CHEESE SANDWICHES

1 (12-ounce) package sharp
  Cheddar cheese, cut into
  1-inch cubes
1 (4-ounce) jar chopped
  pimiento, drained
3 medium-size sweet pickles
½ cup mayonnaise
1 teaspoon sugar
½ teaspoon salt
¼ teaspoon pepper
2 (16-ounce) loaves
  thin-sliced white bread

Position knife blade in processor bowl; add cheese, pimiento, and pickles. Process 5 seconds. Stop processor, and scrape sides of bowl with a rubber spatula. Process 3 to 5 additional seconds. Add remaining ingredients except bread; process 5 seconds or until mixture is well blended. Set aside.

Remove crust from bread, and cut into assorted shapes. Spread filling on half the pieces; top with remaining pieces. Yield: about 2 dozen.

Note: To mix pimiento cheese without the use of a food processor, grate cheese into a medium mixing bowl; add remaining ingredients except bread. Mix at medium speed of an electric mixer until well blended.

CHICKEN SALAD SANDWICHES

¾ cup diced cooked chicken
¾ cup finely chopped celery
2 tablespoons mayonnaise
2 teaspoons lemon juice
Salt to taste
Dash of pepper
12 slices white bread
Lettuce leaves

Combine chicken, celery, mayonnaise, lemon juice, salt, and pepper; mix well.

Remove crust from bread. Spread ¼ cup chicken salad on 6 slices of bread; top each with a lettuce leaf and remaining slices of bread. Cut each sandwich into 3 rectangles. Yield: 1½ dozen.

My head's in a whirl
For you VALENTINE GIRL!
So, Oh! Give me joy
Say "VALENTINE - BOY!

VALENTINE SUGAR COOKIES

1 cup butter or margarine,
  softened
2 cups sugar
3 eggs
1½ tablespoons milk
2 teaspoons vanilla extract
4½ cups all-purpose flour
1 tablespoon baking
  powder
1½ teaspoons salt
¼ teaspoon ground nutmeg
Cherry Frosting
Red decorator sugar crystals

Cream butter; gradually add sugar, beating well. Add eggs, milk, and vanilla; mix well.

Combine dry ingredients; gradually add to creamed mixture, mixing well after each each addition. Divide dough in half.

Roll half of dough to ¼-inch thickness on a lightly floured surface; chill remaining dough. Cut dough with a heart-shaped cookie cutter. Place on lightly greased baking sheets; bake at 375° for 10 minutes or until edges are lightly browned. Cool on a wire rack. Repeat procedure with remaining dough. Frost with Cherry Frosting and sprinkle with sugar crystals. Yield: 3 dozen.

Note: Leftover cookies may be placed in an airtight container and frozen for later use.

Cherry Frosting:

¼ cup plus 2 tablespoons
  butter or margarine,
  softened
1 cup sifted powdered sugar
1 tablespoon maraschino
  cherry juice
2 drops red food coloring

Cream butter; gradually add sugar, beating well. Add cherry juice, mixing until smooth. Stir in food coloring. Yield: enough frosting for 3 dozen cookies.

HOT CHOCOLATE

3 (1-ounce) squares
  semisweet chocolate
½ cup sugar
½ teaspoon salt
2 cups boiling water
6 cups milk, scalded
8 to 16 large marshmallows

Melt chocolate in top of a double boiler over boiling water. Add sugar, salt, and boiling water; stir well. Cook 1 minute; add milk. Beat at medium speed of electric mixer 2 minutes. Pour into mugs and top with marshmallows. Serve immediately. Yield: 8 cups.

Haste makes waste" but I'm
in haste to have YOU waste
your affections on ME

A COLLECTION OF CONFECTIONS

Always around St. Valentine's Day one hears "Sweets to the sweet." And, starting in January, we notice massed displays of heart-shaped, red satin boxes filled with choice chocolates. But Southerners are a funny lot: they like to try to create their own delightful sugarplums for gifts and entertaining. Do, for fun, make "Secrets," a pretty conceit from the century we left behind. The glazed paper may be waxed paper from the shelf, but confectioner's supply houses carry "kiss papers" already cut, as well as colorful bonbon cups. When wrapping "Secrets," it is best not to include Minted Nuts as the mint permeates the other tidbits.

CREAMY PASTEL BONBONS
DATE KISSES ∗ SECRETS
CHOCOLATE-COVERED CHERRIES
MINTED NUTS

Serves 12

CREAMY PASTEL BONBONS

1 (3-ounce) package cream cheese, softened
2 cups sifted powdered sugar
¼ cup cocoa
1 tablespoon plus 1 teaspoon butter or margarine, melted
1 teaspoon vanilla extract
Coating (recipe follows)

Beat cream cheese at medium speed of electric mixer until light and fluffy; gradually add sugar, beating well. Add cocoa, butter, and vanilla; mix well.

Shape mixture into ¾-inch balls, and place on waxed paper. Chill 1 hour.

Using 2 forks, quickly dip balls, one at a time, into warm coating mixture. If necessary to maintain coating consistency, add a small amount of warm milk. Place on waxed paper; refrigerate until coating is firm. Yield: about 1½ dozen.

Coating:

2 cups sifted powdered sugar
2 tablespoons butter or margarine, softened
2 tablespoons milk
½ teaspoon vanilla extract
2 to 3 drops food coloring

Combine sugar, butter, and milk in top of double boiler; place over boiling water. Cook until mixture is smooth. Stir in vanilla and food coloring.

Remove double boiler from heat, leaving coating mixture over hot water. Use immediately. Yield: about 1½ cups.

DATE KISSES

1 egg white
½ cup sifted powdered sugar
½ cup chopped pecans
½ cup chopped dates

Beat egg white (at room temperature) in a medium mixing bowl until stiff peaks form. Gradually add sugar, beating well. Fold in pecans and dates.

Drop by teaspoonfuls onto waxed paper-lined baking sheets. Bake at 250° for 30 to 35 minutes. Cool on baking sheets. Yield: about 3 dozen.

SECRETS

Take glazed paper of different colours and cut into squares of equal size, fringing two sides of each. Have ready burnt almonds, chocolate nuts, bonbons, and sugarplums of various sorts. Put one in each paper with a folded slip containing two lines of verse. Twist the coloured paper so as entirely to conceal their contents, leaving the fringe at each end."

Directions for Cookery, 1837

"I Toast Your Heart, May It Grow Warmer," dated 1912.

CHOCOLATE-COVERED CHERRIES

About 44 maraschino cherries
   with stems
1 (8-ounce) bar milk
   chocolate
4 (1-ounce) squares
   unsweetened chocolate
Cornstarch
Fondant (recipe follows)

Drain cherries; dry on paper towels. Set aside.

Combine milk chocolate and unsweetened chocolate in top of a double boiler; place over water, and bring to a boil. Reduce heat to low; cook until chocolate melts, stirring occasionally.

Remove double boiler from heat, leaving chocolate mixture over hot water.

Dip fingers in cornstarch and shape a small amount of fondant around each cherry. Place on waxed paper-lined baking sheets.

Holding each fondant-coated cherry by the stem, dip in chocolate mixture, allowing excess chocolate to drain back into top of double boiler.

Place cherries on wire racks over waxed paper; refrigerate until chocolate coating has hardened. Store cherries in cool place. Yield: about 3½ dozen.

Note: The flavor of Chocolate Covered Cherries will be enhanced when stored in a tightly covered container up to 2 weeks. The fondant will have mellowed and blended with the flavor of the liqueur.

Fondant:

2 cups sugar
¾ cup water
⅛ teaspoon cream of
   tartar
2 teaspoons kirsch or
   Grand Marnier

Combine sugar and water in a medium saucepan; place over low heat, stirring until sugar is dissolved. Increase heat; continue stirring until mixture comes to a boil. Stir in cream of tartar.

Date Kisses, Chocolate-Covered Cherries, and Minted Nuts.

Wash off crystals that have formed on sides of pan, using a brush dipped in cold water. Cover and boil vigorously for 3 minutes. Uncover; cook rapidly, without stirring, until mixture reaches soft ball stage (240°). Immediately remove from heat; pour mixture out onto a damp counter or marble slab, leaving any crystallized sugar in pan. Let syrup cool.

Using a spatula, pull sides into middle repeatedly until mixture begins to thicken and turn white.

Knead fondant with buttered hands until creamy enough to form a firm ball. Sprinkle with kirsch or Grand Marnier; knead lightly. Store in a tightly covered contained for at least 4 days before using. Yield: enough to coat 44 cherries.

MINTED NUTS

1 cup sugar
½ cup water
1 tablespoon light corn syrup
½ teaspoon salt
6 large marshmallows
3 drops oil of peppermint
3 cups pecan halves

Combine sugar, water, corn syrup, and salt in a small saucepan. Cook over medium heat, stirring constantly, until just before mixture reaches thread stage (230°).

Remove from heat; add marshmallows, stirring until melted. Add oil of peppermint and pecans, stirring to coat well. Place pecans individually on waxed paper; cool completely. Store in an airtight container. Yield: about 3 cups.

Mardi Gras

As the revels of Twelfth Night close out the Christmas holidays, they open up the time of carnival that reaches a crescendo on Shrovetide or Shrove Tuesday. "Shrove" is Anglo-Saxon-English for the Christian tenet that sins be confessed before Lent "and the confessor shrive him." Carnival is from the Latin *carne* (meat) and *vale* (farewell.)

In Germany, Shrove Tuesday is Fastnacht; in France, Mardi Gras, or "Fat Tuesday." The latter refers to the fact that no meat will be eaten during the forty days of Lent, so fats are used up before Ash Wednesday, the first day of Lent.

Of all the mid-winter festivals in the United States, none is more famous than Mardi Gras, the few days of Misrule that crown the New Orleans carnival season. Mobile, Galveston, Pensacola, and Shreveport hold annual festivals too, and other cities in the South have parades and balls on a less regular schedule.

The Crescent City counters that Mardi Gras dates back to 1827, when some young men brought the festival home from France where they had been to school. But it was not until 1857, when the Mystic Krewe of Comus was formed, that New Orleans adopted Mobile's symbolic pageants and elaborate floats. The Rex organization was formed when the Russian Grand Duke Alexis visited New Orleans in 1872. Rex, Lord of Misrule, was King. Official colors of purple, green, and gold, were selected. In the Duke's honor, all the groups of maskers came together for a fantastic parade that became a permanent part of Mardi Gras. It was Alexis who selected the Mardi Gras theme music, "If Ever I Cease To Love." He was smitten by the beauteous actress, Lydia Thompson, who sang it in *Bluebeard*. The music was set to march time, and its strains are known to every bandsman who has ever marched in a Mardi Gras parade.

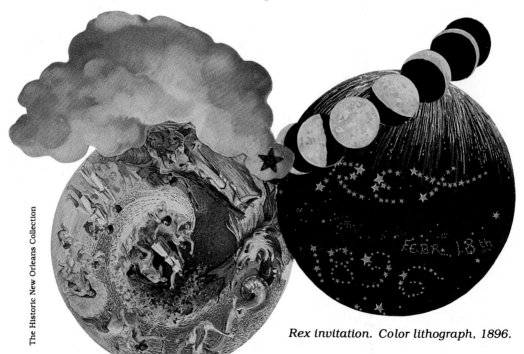

The Historic New Orleans Collection

Rex invitation. Color lithograph, 1896.

Frank
Howard
was Rex
in 1895.

Unicorn float c. 1900

William Pike wore a fake
beard as Rex in 1874.

The first
Mardi Gras
procession—
like this
one c. 1900 —
was in 1857.

KING REX COCKTAIL PARTY

Among the libations offered everywhere in New Orleans during Mardi Gras is Absinthe Frappé. What you will not see is absinthe. Banned in 1912, the greenish anise-flavored liqueur from France or Switzerland contained wormwood, a toxic herb. "Among its effects were derangement of the digestive organs, delirium, and idiocy," and it proved addictive to some.

Absinthe is now used as a generic term for anise-flavored liqueur, such as Pernod, Raki, and Ojen. The latter is short for Bobadillojen, a Spanish product difficult to find, so, again, substitution is likely.

Milk Punch, dating back many centuries, is known for its curative effects.

ABSINTHE FRAPPÉ
BLOODY MARY
NEW ORLEANS MILK PUNCH
MIMOSA * NEGRONI
OJEN COCKTAIL

Serves 1 Beverage for Each Recipe

Cocktails should be made individually to serve any number of guests.

ABSINTHE FRAPPÉ

¼ cup Pernod
½ teaspoon superfine sugar
Ice cubes

Combine Pernod and sugar, stirring well to dissolve sugar. To serve, fill a chilled wine glass with ice; add Pernod mixture. Yield: 1 serving.

BLOODY MARY

½ cup tomato juice
1 tablespoon lemon juice
1 teaspoon Worcestershire sauce
2 to 3 drops hot sauce
Pinch of salt
Pinch of pepper
2 tablespoons vodka
Ice cubes
Lime wedge

Combine first 6 ingredients, mixing well. Stir vodka into tomato juice mixture; pour over ice cubes. Garnish with lime wedge. Yield: 1 serving.

Clockwise from top: Mimosa, Absinthe Frappé, Negroni, Milk Punch, Ojen Cocktail, and Bloody Mary.

Folded view of a Mardi Gras Ball invitation, 1888.

Procession of the "Mistick Krewe of Comus," by James E. Taylor.

NEW ORLEANS MILK PUNCH

¾ cup whipping cream
2 tablespoons plus 1
  teaspoon brandy, chilled
1 teaspoon superfine sugar
⅛ teaspoon vanilla extract
Ground nutmeg

Combine whipping cream, brandy, sugar, and vanilla; stir well. Pour into a chilled glass, and sprinkle with nutmeg. Yield: 1 serving.

MIMOSA

½ cup orange juice, chilled
½ cup brut champagne,
  chilled

Combine orange juice and champagne, stirring well. Serve in a tall champagne glass. Yield: 1 serving.

NEGRONI

1 tablespoon Campari
1 tablespoon gin
1 tablespoon Italian vermouth
Ice cubes

Combine Campari, gin, vermouth; stir well, and serve over ice. Yield: 1 serving.

OJEN COCKTAIL

1½ tablespoons Bobadillojen,
  Anisette, or other
  anise-flavored liqueur
3 dashes bitters

Combine Bobadillojen and bitters, and shake thoroughly with ice. Strain into a chilled glass to serve. Yield: 1 serving.

Note: Anisette is often subsituted for Bobadillojen, an imported Spanish cordial which is not marketed nationwide.

35

MARDI GRAS IN MOBILE

Mobilians will tell you their city not only holds clear title to Mardi Gras, but also is the Mother of Mystics. French under Bienville and Iberville built a fort near present-day Mobile in 1702, celebrated their first Mardi Gras in 1703, and formed the first Mystical Society in 1704. In 1711, on moving to the city's present site, they formed a second Society; the Spaniards added a torchlight parade in 1780.

Mardi Gras languished during the Civil War, but in 1866, the town clerk, Joe Cain, dressed up as an Indian chief and drove about in an old charcoal wagon, cheering and rallying the town. Mobile has a Joe Cain parade in his honor on Mardi Gras Sunday.

COLD BEEF MOLD
CHICKEN SALAD
CHAFING DISH BEEF BARBECUE
CRABMEAT IMPERIAL
MINIATURE COCONUT TARTS
INDIVIDUAL PINEAPPLE CHIFFON PIES
STRAWBERRIES WITH CRÈME FRAÎCHE

Serves 10

COLD BEEF MOLD

1 envelope unflavored gelatin
3 tablespoons boiling water
1 (10-ounce) package frozen English peas
¾ cup commercial sour cream
¾ cup mayonnaise
¼ cup chopped fresh parsley
2 tablespoons chopped green onion
1 tablespoon capers, mashed
1 tablespoon red wine vinegar
1 teaspoon lemon juice
½ teaspoon salt
½ teaspoon pepper
⅛ teaspoon dried whole tarragon
⅛ teaspoon dried whole chervil
¾ pound chopped cooked roast beef
1 cup cooked cubed carrots
Leaf lettuce

Dissolve gelatin in boiling water; set aside.

Cook peas according to package. Drain; set aside to cool.

Combine next 11 ingredients; mix well. Stir in gelatin mixture. Fold in peas, beef, and carrots. Spoon into an oiled 5-cup mold; chill until firm. Unmold on lettuce. Yield: 10 servings.

CHICKEN SALAD

2½ cups chopped cooked chicken
1¾ cups finely chopped celery
2 hard-cooked eggs, chopped
2 tablespoons minced onion
1½ cups mayonnaise
¼ cup sweet pickle relish, drained
2 tablespoons lemon juice
1 teaspoon salt
½ teaspoon pepper

Combine all ingredients; mix well. Cover and chill at least 2 hours. Serve on party bread or crackers. Yield: 10 servings.

The Historic New Orleans Collection

CHAFING DISH BEEF BARBECUE

2½ pounds lean beef for stewing, cut into 1-inch strips
1 (14½-ounce) can whole tomatoes, chopped and undrained
1 medium onion, chopped
2 cups water
½ cup Worcestershire sauce
¼ cup vinegar
4 cloves garlic, minced
½ teaspoon salt
¼ teaspoon pepper
½ teaspoon chili powder
4 drops hot sauce
Small biscuits

Place all ingredients, except biscuits, in a large Dutch oven; bring to a boil. Cover; reduce heat, and simmer 3 hours, stirring occasionally. Remove cover, and continue cooking over low heat 2 hours, stirring occasionally. Place in chafing dish; serve with small biscuits. Yield: 10 servings.

1896 Carnival pin: planet crowned in clouds; phases of moon "in seriatim."

CRABMEAT IMPERIAL

⅓ cup chopped green
  pepper
2 tablespoons chopped
  pimiento, drained
1 teaspoon Dijon mustard
1 teaspoon salt
⅛ teaspoon white pepper
1 egg, beaten
⅓ cup mayonnaise
1 pound fresh crabmeat,
  drained and flaked
10 commercial patty shells,
  baked
Additional mayonnaise
Paprika

Combine first 5 ingredients in
a large bowl. Combine egg and
⅓ cup mayonnaise; stir into
green pepper mixture, mixing
well. Gently stir in crabmeat.

Spoon crabmeat into baked
patty shells. Top each with a
dollop of mayonnaise; sprinkle
with paprika. Bake at 350° for
15 minutes. Yield: 10 servings.

MINIATURE COCONUT
TARTS

1 envelope unflavored
  gelatin
½ cup sugar
⅛ teaspoon salt
3 egg yolks
1¾ cup milk
1 teaspoon vanilla extract
¾ cup flaked coconut
32 baked miniature tart shells
Whipped cream
16 fresh strawberries, halved
  (optional)

Combine gelatin, sugar, and
salt in top of a double boiler.
Combine egg yolks and milk;
mix well. Gradually add to gelatin mixture, stirring well. Place
over boiling water; cook 10 minutes, stirring constantly, until
mixture is thickened. Remove
from heat; stir in vanilla. Set
aside to cool.

Fold coconut into cooled custard. Spoon 1 tablespoon coconut custard into each tart shell.
Top each tart with a dollop of
whipped cream; garnish with
strawberry halves, if desired.
Yield: 32 miniature tarts.

Cold Beef Salad Mold (right front) and Chicken Salad.

INDIVIDUAL
PINEAPPLE CHIFFON
PIES

1 envelope unflavored gelatin
¼ cup cold water
3 eggs, separated
¾ cup sugar, divided
1 (15½-ounce) can crushed
  pineapple, undrained and
  divided
1 teaspoon grated lemon rind
3 tablespoons lemon juice
¼ teaspoon salt
10 (3-inch) baked tart shells
½ cup whipping cream,
  whipped

Sprinkle gelatin over cold
water; let stand 5 minutes.

Combine egg yolks, ¼ cup
sugar, ¾ cup pineapple, lemon
rind, and juice in top of a double
boiler. Place over boiling water
and cook, stirring constantly,
until smooth and thickened.
Add softened gelatin; stir until
gelatin is dissolved. Remove
from heat and cool.

Beat egg whites (at room temperature) and salt until soft
peaks form. Gradually add remaining sugar, beating until
stiff peaks form. Fold into pineapple mixture. Spoon into tart
shells; chill. Garnish with
whipped cream and remaining
pineapple. Yield: 10 servings.

STRAWBERRIES WITH
CRÈME FRAÎCHE

1 cup whipping cream
1 tablespoon buttermilk
1 quart fresh strawberries,
  hulled

Combine cream and butter-
milk in a mixing bowl; cover and
let stand at room temperature
overnight. Chill.

Scrape thickened cream into
a filter paper-lined strainer.
Drain; discard liquid. Chill remaining crème fraîche. Serve as
a dip with fresh strawberries.
Yield: ¾ cup.

CARNIVAL DESSERT PARTY

The Twelfth Night grand balls and revels that launch the carnival season in New Orleans always include the presentation of the Twelfth Night Cake or King's Cake, both of which are baked with a bean inside. The brioche-like yeast cake is shaped into an oval ring to resemble a crown and bejeweled with dragees, caramels, and sugars in the colors of carnival.

Throughout carnival, by old custom, the King Cake is baked each week, a fresh one supplied by the out-going monarchs, until the final strains of "If Ever I Cease To Love" have died away.

KING CAKE
PECAN LACE COOKIES
OREILLES DE COCHON (Pig's Ears)
PRALINE BREAD
MINIATURE CREAM PUFFS
COFFEE WITH ASSORTED LIQUEURS

Serves 16

KING CAKE

½ cup warm water (105°
  to 115°)
2 packages dry yeast
2 teaspoons sugar
4 to 5 cups all-purpose flour,
  divided
½ cup sugar
2 teaspoons salt
1 teaspoon ground nutmeg
1 teaspoon grated lemon rind
½ cup warm milk (105° to
  115°)
½ cup butter or margarine,
  melted
5 egg yolks
½ cup finely chopped candied
  citron (optional)
1 dried bean or pecan half
Glaze (recipe follows)
Purple, green, and gold
  sugar crystals

Combine water, yeast, and 2 teaspoons sugar in a small bowl. Mix well; let stand 5 minutes or until bubbly.

Combine 4 cups flour, ½ cup sugar, salt, nutmeg, and lemon rind; add warm milk, melted butter, egg yolks, and yeast mixture. Beat until smooth.

Turn dough out onto a lightly floured surface; knead in enough remaining flour to make a stiff dough. Continue kneading 8 to 10 minutes or until dough is smooth and elastic.

Place dough in a greased bowl, turning to grease top. Cover and let rise in a warm place (85°), free from drafts, 1 hour or until doubled in bulk. Punch dough down, and place on a lightly floured surface. Sprinkle with citron, if desired, and knead until citron is evenly distributed. Shape dough into a cylinder 30 inches long.

Place cylinder on a greased baking sheet; shape into a ring, pinching ends together to seal. Place a well-greased 2-pound coffee can in center of ring to maintain shape during baking.

Press bean or pecan gently into ring from bottom so it is completely hidden by dough. Cover ring with a towel, and repeat rising procedure 45 minutes or until doubled in bulk.

Bake at 350° for 25 minutes or until golden brown. Remove coffee can and place cake on wire rack to cool. Drizzle cake with glaze; sprinkle with sugar crystals, alternating colors. Yield: 16 to 18 servings.

Glaze:

2 cups sifted powdered sugar
2 tablespoons lemon juice
1 tablespoon water

Combine all ingredients and beat until smooth. Yield: about 1½ cups.

PECAN LACE COOKIES

Butter or margarine
All-purpose flour
2 tablespoons butter or
  margarine, softened
2 cups sugar
2 eggs
1 teaspoon vanilla extract
½ cup all-purpose flour
1 teaspoon baking powder
Pinch of salt
2 cups chopped pecans

Grease baking sheets with butter, and dust with flour.

Cream 2 tablespoons butter; gradually add sugar, beating well. Add eggs and vanilla; mix well. Combine ½ cup flour, baking powder, and salt; add to creamed mixture, mixing well. Fold in pecans.

Drop batter by teaspoonfuls, 3 inches apart, onto prepared baking sheets; bake at 400° for 3 minutes or until edges are lightly browned. Cool slightly before removing to wire racks to cool completely. Yield: about 3 dozen.

From King Cake (top right) clockwise: sliced Praline Bread, Miniature Cream Puffs, Pecan Lace Cookies, and Oreilles de Cochon.

OREILLES DE COCHON

½ cup butter or margarine
2 cups all-purpose flour
2 teaspoons baking powder
½ teaspoon salt
2 eggs
Vegetable oil
2 cups cane syrup
1 cup coarsely chopped
    pecans

Melt butter in a heavy sauce-pan over low heat; let cool.

Sift together flour, baking powder, and salt; set aside.

Beat eggs in a large mixing bowl until light and frothy. Continue beating, and gradually add melted butter. Stir in flour mixture, mixing well, to form a dough.

Divide dough into 16 equal portions, rolling each portion into a ball. Roll each ball out into an 8-inch circle on a lightly floured surface.

Heat 1½ to 2 inches of oil to 375° in a medium skillet. Drop a pastry circle into hot oil using a long-handled fork; immediately stick the fork tines in the center of the pastry, and twist quickly. Hold with fork until set (pastry will fold over on itself, forming an "ear"); cook until golden brown on both sides. Drain on paper towels. Repeat procedure with remaining pastry.

Pour syrup into a heavy saucepan; bring to a boil. Cook 5 minutes, stirring constantly. Dip each pastry in hot syrup, coating well on both sides. Sprinkle with pecans; let dry on buttered waxed paper. Yield: 16 pastries.

PRALINE BREAD

½ cup chopped pecans
¾ cup praline liqueur, divided
½ cup butter or margarine,
    softened
1 cup firmly packed brown
    sugar
1½ teaspoons vanilla extract
3 eggs
¼ cup milk
2 cups all-purpose flour
¼ teaspoon baking powder
1 teaspoon ground cinnamon

Combine pecans and ¼ cup praline liqueur; cover and set aside overnight.

Cream butter; gradually add sugar, beating well. Add vanilla; beat well. Add eggs and milk, beating well.

Combine flour, baking powder, and cinnamon; add to creamed mixture, stirring well. Stir in pecan mixture. Pour batter into 2 greased 7½- x 3- x 2-inch loafpans. Bake at 325° for 55 minutes or until a wooden pick inserted in center comes out clean. Cool in pans 10 minutes. Remove from pans; place on wire racks to cool completely.

Drizzle ¼ cup praline liqueur evenly over each cooled loaf. Wrap each loaf in cheesecloth; cover tightly in aluminum foil. Allow to season for 3 days before serving. Yield: 2 loaves.

MINIATURE CREAM PUFFS

1 cup water
½ cup butter or margarine
¼ teaspoon salt
1 cup all-purpose flour
4 eggs
Filling (recipe follows)
Frosting (recipes follows)

Combine water and butter in a medium saucepan; bring to a boil. Add salt and flour, all at once, stirring vigorously over low heat until mixture leaves sides of pan and forms a smooth ball. Remove from heat, and cool slightly.

Add eggs, one at a time, beating well after each addition; beat until batter is smooth.

Drop batter by rounded tea-spoonfuls, 3 inches apart, onto greased baking sheets. Bake at 425° for 15 minutes or until puffed and golden brown. Remove to wire racks, and cool away from drafts.

Cut tops off cream puffs; pull out and discard soft dough inside. Fill bottom halves with filling; replace top, and spread frosting on top half. Serve immediately or refrigerate. Yield: about 3½ dozen.

Filling:

3½ tablespoons all-purpose
    flour
1⅓ cups sugar
Dash of salt
3 egg yolks, beaten
3 cups milk
1 teaspoon vanilla
    extract

Combine flour, sugar, and salt in a heavy saucepan. Combine egg yolks and milk, mixing well. Stir into dry ingredients; cook over medium heat, stirring constantly, until smooth and thickened. Remove from heat; stir in vanilla. Chill thoroughly. Yield: about 5 cups.

Frosting:

½ cup butter or margarine,
    softened
2 tablespoons plus 2
    teaspoons milk
4 cups sifted powdered sugar
Green, purple, and orange
    paste food coloring

Cream butter; add milk, mixing well. Gradually add sugar, beating well. Divide frosting into thirds. Add food coloring to each portion to desired color. Yield: enough frosting for 3½ dozen miniature cream puffs.

St.Patrick's Day

St. Patrick was born near Dumbarton, Scotland in 387 A.D.. At age sixteen, the youth was captured by Irish marauders and sold as a slave to a Druid chief in Ireland. For six years he worked as a swineherd and mastered the Celtic language before escaping back to Scotland.

He entered religious life at the monastery of St. Martin at Tours, France. In his eighteen years there, he became a priest, then a bishop. He was sent back to Ireland in 432 by Pope Celestine I. Patricius, as the Pope named him, was not welcomed kindly by the Druids. But eventually he purchased his freedom from his former owner and converted him and his family to Christianity.

For thirty years Patricius labored among the Irish in spite of many persecutions. The shamrock evolved as the national symbol of Ireland because Patricius used it to illustrate the concept of the Holy Trinity. He died on March 17, 463 (or 465), leaving us to wonder if he really did drive the snakes out of Ireland.

Wearing the green, pretty Colleen carries a pot of shamrocks, symbol of Erin. St. Patrick's Day greeting card, 1908.

ST. PADDY'S DAY IN SAVANNAH

avannah's Hibernian Society has been keeping St. Patrick's Day since 1812, and long practice has made their celebration one of the South's most notable.

This Savannah-Irish dinner characterizes the simplicity of traditional Irish food. Along with potatoes ("praties"), Soda Bread is one of Ireland's staple foods. And if we suspect that it is just like a big buttermilk biscuit, we won't be far off although there are variations. But it is baked in a round loaf with a cross cut into the top, which divides it into quarters, or "farls." And, as a final Irish treat, there's Tea Brack with your "cuppa."

SAVANNAH CORNED BEEF DINNER
or
BOILED CORNED BEEF DINNER
IRISH SODA BREAD
IRISH TEA BRACK
BEER

Serves 8 to 10

SAVANNAH CORNED BEEF DINNER

1 (4- to 5-pound) corned beef brisket, trimmed
2 bay leaves
1½ teaspoons whole cloves
1½ teaspoons whole peppercorns
1 medium cabbage, cut into wedges
6 medium potatoes, peeled and cubed
6 medium carrots, scraped and cut in julienne strips
4 medium onions, peeled and quartered
Fresh parsley sprigs (optional)

Place brisket in a large Dutch oven; cover with water. Add spices. Bring to a boil and cover; reduce heat, and simmer for 2½ hours or until brisket is tender.

Add cabbage; cover and simmer 10 minutes. Add potatoes, carrots, and onions; cover and simmer an additional 20 minutes or until vegetables are tender.

Remove brisket to a warm platter; slice thinly across the grain. Remove vegetables from liquid, discarding spices; place on platter with sliced brisket. Garnish with parsley, if desired. Yield: 8 to 10 servings.

St. Pat's Day Savannah Corned Beef Dinner, ready to cook.

Dressing up for St. Patrick's Day. John Reid, 1872.

BOILED CORNED BEEF DINNER

1 (2½-pound) corned beef brisket
5 carrots, scraped and cut into 1-inch pieces
3 stalks celery, cut into ½-inch pieces
1 large onion, cut into thin slices
1 bay leaf
½ teaspoon garlic powder
1½ cups quick barley

Place brisket in a Dutch oven; add water to cover. Bring to a boil and cover; reduce heat, and simmer for 3 hours or until brisket is tender. Remove brisket from pan, and strain broth.

Return brisket and strained broth to Dutch oven. Add next 5 ingredients. Bring to a boil and cover; reduce heat, and simmer 30 minutes. Add barley; cook an additional 30 minutes.

Remove brisket to a serving platter; slice thinly across the grain. Drain vegetable and barley mixture, discarding bay leaf, and serve with brisket. Yield: 8 to 10 servings.

IRISH SODA BREAD

1 cup sifted all-purpose flour
2 teaspoons baking soda
1½ teaspoons salt
¼ cup butter or margarine, softened
3 cups whole wheat flour
1⅔ cups buttermilk

Sift together all-purpose flour, baking soda, and salt in a large mixing bowl. Cut in butter with a pastry blender until mixture resembles coarse meal. Stir in whole wheat flour, mixing well. Add buttermilk, stirring until the dry ingredients are thoroughly moistened.

Turn dough out onto a lightly floured surface, and knead about 5 minutes. Shape dough into a round loaf; place on a greased baking sheet. Using a sharp knife, cut a cross ¼-inch deep on top of loaf; lightly sprinkle cross with flour.

Bake at 400° for 40 minutes or until bread sounds hollow when tapped. Remove from baking sheet, and cool completely on wire rack. Yield: 1 loaf.

IRISH TEA BRACK

½ cup dried peaches, chopped
½ cup dried apricots, chopped
½ cup dried prunes, chopped
1 cup hot, strong tea
1 cup sugar
1 egg, beaten
1 tablespoon orange marmalade
1 teaspoon pumpkin pie spice
1¾ cups self-rising flour
Butter or margarine (optional)

Combine dried fruit and tea in a large bowl; cover and let stand overnight.

Add next 3 ingredients to fruit mixture; stir well. Gradually add flour, mixing well.

Spoon batter into a greased 9-inch square pan. Bake at 350° for 35 minutes or until a wooden pick inserted in center comes out clean. Cut into squares. Serve with butter, if desired. Yield: 8 to 10 servings.

A GREAT DAY FOR THE IRISH

S t. Patrick's Day in Dublin, Georgia, proves that a tradition does not have to be terribly old to be terribly good. The celebration-come-lately, inaugurated in 1966, quickly became a Springtime highlight for the little city on the Oconee River.

We note again in this traditional menu the prevalence of root vegetables and cabbage in the Irish diet. And nothing could be more Irish than cooking a stew in a Dutch oven. The old Irish version of the Dutch oven was called the "oven-pot," or *bastible*. It came with a concave lid on which to pile the hot turf (peat) used for fuel.

IRISH BEEF STEW
COLE SLAW
IRISH SODA BREAD
(Recipe on page 43)
SPICE CUPCAKES

Serves 8 to 10

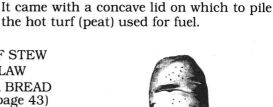

IRISH BEEF STEW

3 pounds lean beef for stewing, cut into 1-inch cubes
3 tablespoons vegetable oil
1 tablespoon lemon-pepper marinade
1 teaspoon garlic powder
1 teaspoon dried whole oregano
1 teaspoon paprika
½ teaspoon ground ginger
½ teaspoon ground nutmeg
4 beef bouillon cubes
4 cups hot water
1 cup Burgundy or other dry red wine
8 medium carrots, scraped and cut into 1-inch thick slices
8 medium Irish potatoes, peeled and cut into 1-inch cubes
4 stalks celery, cut into 1-inch pieces
4 medium onions, coarsely chopped

Brown beef in oil in a large Dutch oven over medium heat. Drain off any excess oil. Stir in spices, bouillon cubes, water, and wine. Bring to a boil and cover; reduce heat and simmer 30 minutes.

Add vegetables; cover and simmer 1½ hours. Yield: 8 to 10 servings.

COLE SLAW

8 cups shredded cabbage
½ cup vinegar
¼ cup plus 2 tablespoons sugar
2 tablespoons chopped onion
1 teaspoon salt
⅔ cup vegetable oil
Paprika
Chopped fresh parsley

Combine first 6 ingredients; toss lightly to coat cabbage. Cover and refrigerate overnight. Garnish with paprika and parsley. Yield: 8 to 10 servings.

SPICE CUPCAKES

1 cup butter or margarine, softened
1¼ cups firmly packed brown sugar
2 eggs
2⅓ cups all-purpose flour
1 teaspoon baking powder
1 teaspoon baking soda
1 teaspoon salt
1½ teaspoons ground cinnamon
1 teaspoon ground ginger
½ teaspoon ground allspice
½ teaspoon ground cloves
1 cup milk
Lemon Frosting
Grated lemon rind

Cream butter; gradually add sugar, beating well. Add eggs; beat well.

Combine flour, baking powder, soda, salt, and spices; add to creamed mixture alternately with milk, beginning and ending with flour mixture.

Spoon batter into greased muffin pans. Bake at 350° for 20 to 25 minutes. Remove to wire racks to cool completely. Frost with Lemon Frosting, and sprinkle with grated lemon rind. Yield: about 2 dozen.

Lemon Frosting:

¼ cup plus 2 tablespoons butter or margarine, softened
3¼ cups sifted powdered sugar, divided
¼ cup lemon juice
6 drops yellow food coloring

Cream butter; add 1 cup sugar, beating well at medium speed of electric mixer. Add remaining sugar alternately with lemon juice, beating until smooth enough to spread. Stir in food coloring. Yield: enough for 2 dozen cupcakes.

Suitable fare for St. Patrick's Day, Dublin, Georgia. Irish Beef Stew, Spice Cupcakes, Cole Slaw.

WEARIN' OF THE GREEN IN TEXAS

Dublin, Texas, is another Southern town named for that unique city on the Liffey River, the Dublin that means "Black Pool" for the part of the stream on which it was built. But the Texas town puts on a St. Patrick's bash that is more secular than old Dublin's. Perhaps if you are not in the area, you might visit Shamrock, Texas, which also celebrates its heritage on March 17.

The 1983 "Experience Ireland" Celebration of Dublin included an Irish stew-making contest. Lamb Stew emerged the winner, a proper "white" stew in that the meat is not browned.

Irish stews evolved in the same way our Colonial stews did, with a kettle, a fire, and some meat. Authentic Irish stew, according to purists, is twice as much potato and half as much onion as meat.

IRELAND LAMB STEW
WHISKEY SODA BREAD
HOT IRISH
IRISH FESTIVE CAKE

Serves 8 to 10

IRELAND LAMB STEW

3 to 3½ pounds boneless lamb
2½ teaspoons salt
¼ teaspoon pepper
3 cups water
3 potatoes, peeled and cubed
2 onions, coarsely chopped
3 chicken-flavored bouillon cubes
1 bay leaf, crushed
¼ teaspoon ground allspice
¼ teaspoon garlic salt
1 (10-ounce) package frozen English peas, thawed

Remove fell (tissue-like covering) from lamb; cut meat into 1½-inch cubes. Combine lamb, salt, pepper, and water in a large Dutch oven. Bring to a boil and cover; reduce heat and simmer 20 minutes.

Add remaining ingredients except peas; cover and simmer 1 hour or until potatoes are tender. Add peas, stirring gently; cook until thoroughly heated. Remove bay leaf before serving. Yield: about 9 cups.

In Shamrock, Texas, they dressed for the "Best Costume" award and won!

WHISKEY SODA BREAD

1 cup raisins
½ cup Irish whiskey
3 cups all-purpose flour
½ cup sugar
1 tablespoon baking powder
1 teaspoon salt
1 tablespoon grated orange
  rind
½ teaspoon baking soda
1⅓ cups buttermilk
¼ cup butter or margarine,
  melted
Whiskey Butter

Soak raisins in Irish whiskey overnight.

Combine flour, sugar, baking powder, salt, and orange rind in a large bowl; mix well. Stir in raisin mixture, blending well.

Dissolve soda in buttermilk; add to flour mixture, stirring well. Stir in butter, mixing well.

Spoon batter into a greased 2-quart casserole. Bake at 350° for 50 minutes or until golden brown. Cut into squares, and serve with Whiskey Butter. Yield: 8 to 10 servings.

Whiskey Butter:

½ cup butter or margarine,
  softened
1 tablespoon Irish whiskey

Combine butter and whiskey, blending well. Yield: ½ cup.

HOT IRISH

1 cup hot water
2½ tablespoons Irish whiskey
1 teaspoon brown sugar
1 lemon slice studded with
  cloves

Combine all ingredients in a mug, stirring well. Serve at once. Yield: 1 serving.

Whiskey Soda Bread and butter plus...!

IRISH FESTIVE CAKE

1 (15-ounce) package golden
  raisins
1 (10-ounce) package currants
½ (8-ounce) package candied
  red cherries, chopped
½ (4-ounce) package chopped
  candied lemon peel
½ (4-ounce) package candied
  orange peel
1 cup brandy
1½ cups butter or margarine,
  softened
1½ cups sugar
7 eggs
3½ cups all-purpose flour
½ teaspoon ground cinnamon
½ teaspoon ground nutmeg
2 cups coarsely chopped
  pecans

Combine fruit and brandy in a large bowl. Cover and soak overnight.

Cream butter in a large mixing bowl; gradually add sugar, beating well. Add eggs, one at a time, beating well after each addition.

Combine flour, cinnamon, and nutmeg; gradually add to creamed mixture, mixing well. Stir in fruit-brandy mixture and pecans.

Spoon batter into a paper-lined and greased 10-inch tube pan. Bake at 250° for 3 hours; reduce heat to 150°, and continue baking an additional hour or until a wooden pick inserted in center comes out clean.

Cool in pan; cover and let stand overnight. Remove from pan; cover tightly and store until serving time. Yield: one 10-inch cake.

Easter & Passover

Northern Europeans once had an April festival for Eostre, goddess of fertility and deity of Spring. Sacred fires were set ablaze in her honor, as earth took on new life. Ancient Romans at the same time celebrated a Feast of the Vernal Equinox. When the Saxons became converts to Christianity, they gave Eostre's name to the day set aside to commemorate Christ's rising from the dead, the day we know as Easter.

Gradually old pagan Spring festivals were interwoven with the Christian one. The symbolic use of eggs at Easter goes back to the worship of nature, man's oldest form of wisdom. When primitive people saw an egg hatch and become a living thing, they couldn't have been more astonished if a stone had done so. From inert to living; it had to be a miraculous, awe-inspiring sight. Particularly in cold climates, when winter's desolation gave way to signs of earth's coming back to life, man needed explanations. Small wonder that the egg took on the mystical significance of new life. The egg is tied in with our Easter also because originally it was forbidden to eat them during Lent.

For over three centuries after Christ's death, there raged a controversy as to when Easter should be observed. The resurrection occurred on a Monday, during the Jewish Passover. For Jewish converts, it was simply a matter of two holy days occurring simultaneously. But Gentile converts insisted upon a Sunday. It was they who began celebrating the event with joyful processions and demonstrations not unlike the old rites with which they had welcomed Spring.

In 325 A.D., Constantine the Great, the first Christian Roman Emperor, convened the Church Council at Nicea. One of the matters with which they dealt was dating Easter. They went so far as to name March 21 as the time of the Vernal Equinox, allowing Easter to remain a moveable feast. Now, despite centuries of discussions, Easter can still fall on any Sunday between March 22 and April 25.

As Christianity spread, different countries developed distinctive customs for Easter. Italy and Greece engaged in games and athletic contests. In old Russia, anyone could enter the church and ring the bells. Interestingly, in France, Easter is *Pasque*, from the Latin *Paschalia*, derived from the Hebrew word for Passover, a reminder that Easter and Passover were once observed at the same time.

Lilies, eggs, and children, symbols of "The Dawn of Easter," 1899 stereograph.

MORAVIAN EASTER SUNRISE BREAKFAST

Winston-Salem, North Carolina, has earned the nickname "The Easter City," because the Moravian community there celebrates what many believe is the most beautiful Easter service in the nation. Before dawn on Easter morning, the congregation assembles at the Home Moravian Church in Old Salem to hear the pastor proclaim, "The Lord is risen!"

During the service comes the time appointed for the lovefeast, their ancient expression of Christian unity. The traditional fare is lightly sweetened buns and mugs of coffee containing cream and sugar.

LOVEFEAST BUNS
LOVEFEAST COFFEE
MORAVIAN SUGAR CAKE

Serves 12

LOVEFEAST BUNS

1 package dry yeast
1 cup sugar, divided
¼ cup warm water (105°
 to 115°)
1 egg, beaten
¼ cup butter or margarine,
 softened
¼ cup cooked, mashed
 potatoes
1 teaspoon salt
2 cups warm water (105°
 to 115°)
7 to 8 cups sifted all-purpose
 flour
¼ cup butter or margarine,
 melted

Combine yeast, 1 teaspoon sugar, and ¼ cup warm water; stir well, and let stand 5 minutes or until bubbly.

Combine egg, remaining sugar, softened butter, potatoes, and salt in a large mixing bowl; beat at medium speed of electric mixer 5 minutes or until smooth. Stir in yeast mixture. Add 2 cups warm water alternately with enough flour to make a soft dough, beginning and ending with flour.

Turn dough out onto a lightly floured surface, and knead 10 minutes or until smooth and elastic. Place in a greased bowl, turning to grease top. Cover and let rise in a warm place (85°), free from drafts, 1 hour or until doubled in bulk.

Moravian Lovefeast Buns and Sugar Cake go with coffee.

Punch dough down; shape dough into 3½-inch balls, and place 2 inches apart on greased baking sheets. Cover and repeat rising procedure 1 hour or until doubled in bulk.

Using a sharp knife, cut a shallow "M" on the top of each bun. Bake at 400° for 20 minutes or until golden brown. Brush tops with melted butter. Yield: about 2 dozen.

Men traditionally serve Lovefeast Coffee.
Below: Home Moravian Church.

LOVEFEAST COFFEE

1¼ cups regular grind coffee
3 quarts water
1 cup sugar
1 cup milk

Place coffee grounds in a cheesecloth bag; tightly secure top of bag. Place coffee bag and water in a small Dutch oven; bring to a boil and remove from heat. Stir well. Cover and let stand 15 minutes. Remove coffee bag and discard. Add sugar, and stir until sugar is dissolved. Add milk, stirring well. Serve immediately. Yield: about 12 cups.

MORAVIAN SUGAR CAKE

2 packages dry yeast
⅓ cup plus ½ teaspoon sugar, divided
1 cup warm water (105° to 115°)
3 cups all-purpose flour
¼ cup plus 2 tablespoons instant potato flakes
2 tablespoons instant nonfat dry milk powder
¾ teaspoon salt
2 eggs
½ cup butter or margarine, softened
2 tablespoons milk
½ cup butter or margarine, melted
⅔ cup firmly packed brown sugar
1 teaspoon ground cinnamon

Dissolve yeast and ½ teaspoon sugar in warm water in a large bowl. Add remaining ⅓ cup sugar, 2 cups flour, potato flakes, milk powder, salt, eggs, and ½ cup butter; beat at medium speed of an electric mixer 5 minutes or until smooth. Stir in remaining flour to make a soft dough (dough will be sticky).

Place dough in a greased bowl, turning to grease top. Cover and let rise in a warm place (85°), free from drafts, 1 hour or until doubled in bulk. Stir dough down; cover and refrigerate 30 minutes. Stir dough down again; cover and refrigerate overnight.

Stir dough down and turn onto a greased 15- x 10- x 1-inch jellyroll pan; press dough gently with lightly floured hands to spread evenly over pan. Cover and repeat rising procedure 1 hour or until doubled in bulk.

Brush milk gently over surface of dough. Combine melted butter, brown sugar, and cinnamon; mix well. Pour mixture evenly over surface of dough. Bake at 375° for 15 minutes or until the top is lightly browned. Cool cake slightly, and cut into squares. Yield: one 15- x 10-inch coffee cake.

EASTER EGGS

Long before there was an Easter, eggs were colored, exchanged, and eaten as part of the rites of spring. Brightly colored eggs enchanted cultures from Persia to Greece, from Rome to Europe. Natural dyestuffs have been made from onion skins, flower petals, herbs, spinach, berries, tea, and coffee, to name a few. Bright calicos, tightly wrapped around the egg before cooking, produce beautiful patterns.

Egg decorating in Russia reached a peak when Tzar Nicholas II ordered the court jeweler, Faberge, to make jeweled, golden eggs for the Tzarina. The Ukrainian easter eggs called *pysanky* were (and are) works of art, valued and displayed as any other treasure.

HOMEMADE CANDY EASTER EGGS
NATURAL-DYE EASTER EGGS

Egg rolling on White House lawn, 1901.

Library of Congress

HOMEMADE CANDY EASTER EGGS

8 cups powdered sugar, sifted
1 cup butter or margarine, softened
1 tablespoon maraschino cherry juice
1 cup black walnuts, finely chopped
1 (3-ounce) can flaked coconut
1 (6-ounce) bottle maraschino cherries, drained and finely chopped
1 tablespoon vanilla extract
3 (8-ounce) bars milk chocolate
4 (1-ounce) squares unsweetened chocolate
Royal Frosting

Combine first 3 ingredients in a large mixing bowl; beat until light and fluffy. Add walnuts, coconut, cherries, and vanilla; mix well. Shape dough into 66 ovals about 1½-inches long; place on waxed paper-lined baking sheets, and chill overnight.

Place chocolate in top of a double boiler over hot water, stirring until chocolate melts. Using 2 forks, quickly dip each candy oval into chocolate mixture; return to baking sheet.

Chill until chocolate is firm; store in a cool place. Decorate with Royal Frosting. Yield: 5½ dozen.

Royal Frosting:

3 egg whites
½ teaspoon cream of tartar
1 (16-ounce) package powdered sugar, sifted
Paste food coloring, assorted colors

Combine egg whites (at room temperature) and cream of tartar in a mixing bowl. Beat at medium speed of electric mixer until frothy. Add half of sugar, mixing well. Add remaining sugar; beat at high speed 5 to 7 minutes or until mixture is stiff and holds a peak.

Divide frosting according to the number of different tints desired; add paste food coloring. Frosting dries quickly; keep containers covered with damp towels. Yield: about 2 cups.

Note: For large Candy Easter Eggs, shape dough into 18 ovals about 4 inches long. Decorate with Royal Frosting; personalize each egg with a child's name.

NATURAL-DYE EASTER EGGS

24 hard-cooked eggs, cooled
¼ cup plus 2 tablespoons vinegar, divided
3 (10-ounce) packages frozen raspberries, thawed
2 (16-ounce) cans blueberries, undrained
2 cups strong coffee
Skins of 6 large yellow onions

Have eggs prepared, and pour vinegar in a small bowl.

Pink dye: Strain raspberries, reserving 2 cups juice. Reserve berries for use in another recipe. Bring juice to a boil in a medium saucepan. Remove from heat; add 2 tablespoons vinegar to juice, stirring well. Add 5 eggs, and let stand in dye mixture, turning frequently, until desired pink color is reached. Using a slotted spoon, transfer eggs from dye mixture to paper towels. Let dry completely at room temperature.

Blue dye: Repeat above procedure with blueberries and 5 additional eggs to obtain desired shade of blue.

Beige dye: Place strong coffee in a medium saucepan; bring to a boil. Remove from heat; add 2 tablespoons vinegar to coffee. Add 4 eggs; let stand in dye mixture, turning frequently until desired beige color is reached. Repeat drying procedure.

Yellow dye: Combine onion skins and 2 cups water in a medium saucepan; bring to a boil. Remove from heat. Remove skins from liquid and discard. Add 5 eggs to hot liquid; let stand in dye mixture, turning frequently, until desired yellow color is reached. Repeat drying procedure.

Green dye: Place remaining 5 hard-cooked eggs in blueberry dye mixture. Let stand 1 minute, turning to coat evenly. Using a slotted spoon, transfer blue eggs to yellow onion dye mixture. Let eggs stand in dye mixture, turning frequently, until desired green color is reached. Repeat drying procedure. Yield: 2 dozen dyed eggs.

"Wishing You Every Easter Blessing," late 1800s.

Collection of Business Americana

EASTER SUNDAY DINNER

It is difficult to realize that, early in this country's history, both Easter and Christmas were largely ignored. Puritans from England brought an austere attitude toward these holidays. Louisiana and Maryland, settled by Catholics, were exceptions; but today, every ethnic background is represented in the South's observances.

Children awake on Easter morning and rush to find what goodies the Easter Bunny has hidden. But everyone saves room for the feast that highlights the celebration.

BAKED HAM IN PASTRY
APPLE ASPIC
PICKLED PEACHES
SPINACH CASSEROLE
FROZEN FRUIT SALAD
STRAWBERRY SHORTCAKE

Serves 12

BAKED HAM IN PASTRY

Pastry (recipe follows)
1 (15-pound) uncooked ham
1 quart water
½ cup cider vinegar
1 medium onion, quartered
1 stalk celery, cut into 2-inch pieces
2 bay leaves
1 clove garlic, minced
Pinch of ground thyme
2 teaspoons ground cinnamon
1 teaspoon ground cloves
1 teaspoon ground allspice
½ teaspoon ground nutmeg
1 tablespoon prepared mustard
Apple Aspic (optional)
Watercress (optional)

Prepare pastry, and chill at least 2 hours.

Place ham in a very large container; cover with cold water. Soak ham overnight.

Scrub ham thoroughly with a stiff brush; place, skin side down, in a deep roasting pan. Add water, vinegar, onion, celery, bay leaves, garlic, and thyme. Bake, uncovered, at 350° for 3 hours, basting every 30 minutes with pan drippings.

Carefully remove ham from pan drippings; discard pan drippings. Cool ham, and remove skin. Combine cinnamon, cloves, allspice, and nutmeg, stirring well. Coat ham with spice mixture, and rub evenly with mustard. Set aside.

Roll pastry to ¼-inch thickness on a lightly floured surface. Place prepared ham, flat side up, on pastry. Brush edges of pastry with cold water to seal. Fold pastry around ham, trimming excess pastry, if necessary; pinch edges of pastry together to seal.

Place ham, seam side down, in a lightly greased, shallow roasting pan. Prick entire surface of pastry at 1-inch intervals with a fork. Return ham to oven; bake, covered, at 350° for 1 hour. Uncover and bake an additional 40 minutes or until pastry is lightly browned. Allow ham to cool before slicing.

Transfer to serving platter, and garnish with Apple Aspic and watercress, if desired. Yield: 24 to 30 servings.

Pastry:

6 cups all-purpose flour
2 tablespoons baking powder
1 teaspoon salt
½ cup shortening
2 cups ice water

Combine flour, baking powder, and salt in a large bowl; cut in shortening with a pastry blender until mixture resembles coarse meal. Sprinkle ice water evenly over surface; stir with a fork until dry ingredients are moistened. Shape dough into a ball. Yield: enough for 1 (15-pound) ham.

EASTER GREETING

APPLE ASPIC

1 envelope unflavored gelatin
½ cup cold water
1¼ cups apple juice

Soften gelatin in cold water. Bring apple juice to a boil; remove from heat and add softened gelatin, stirring until dissolved. Pour into a lightly oiled 13- x 9- x 2-inch baking pan; chill until firm. Remove from pan; place in a small mixing bowl and finely chop. Use as a garnish for baked ham. Yield: about 1 cup.

SPINACH CASSEROLE

8 pounds fresh spinach
2 tablespoons butter or margarine
2 tablespoons all-purpose flour
2 cups half-and-half
⅛ teaspoon salt
⅛ teaspoon pepper
4 cups (16 ounces) shredded, sharp Cheddar cheese
1 cup soft breadcrumbs

Remove stems from spinach; wash leaves thoroughly in lukewarm water. Place in a large Dutch oven (do not add water). Cover and cook over high heat 3 to 5 minutes. Drain spinach well; chop and set aside.

Melt butter in a medium saucepan over low heat; add flour, stirring until smooth. Cook 1 minute, stirring constantly. Gradually add half-and-half; cook over medium heat, stirring constantly, until thickened and bubbly. Stir in salt and pepper. Add spinach and cheese; mix well.

Spoon mixture into a greased 2-quart casserole; sprinkle with breadcrumbs. Bake, uncovered, at 350° for 10 to 15 minutes. Yield: 12 servings.

For Easter: Baked Ham in Pastry with Apple Aspic and Pickled Peaches as garnish.

FROZEN FRUIT SALAD

2 (3-ounce) packages cream cheese, softened
⅔ cup mayonnaise
¼ cup whipping cream
¼ cup lemon juice
2 (15½-ounce) cans crushed pineapple, drained
2 cups Royal Anne cherries, pitted and chopped
1 cup chopped pecans
2 cups whipping cream, whipped
Lettuce leaves

Beat cream cheese until smooth; add mayonnaise, ¼ cup whipping cream, and lemon juice, mixing well. Stir in pineapple, cherries, and pecans. Gently fold in whipped cream. Pour mixture into a 13- x 9- x 2-inch baking dish; freeze overnight or until firm.

Place salad in refrigerator for 10 minutes before serving. Cut into squares, and serve on lettuce leaves. Yield: 12 servings.

STRAWBERRY SHORTCAKE

1½ quarts fresh strawberries, halved
¼ to ½ cup sugar
3 cups all-purpose flour
1½ teaspoons salt
1 cup plus 3 tablespoons shortening
½ cup plus 1 tablespoon ice water
1 cup whipping cream
¼ cup sifted powdered sugar
Whole strawberries

Combine halved strawberries and ¼ to ½ cup sugar, stirring gently; chill 1 to 2 hours.

Combine flour and salt in a large mixing bowl; cut in shortening with a pastry blender until mixture resembles coarse meal. Sprinkle ice water evenly over surface; stir with a fork until dry ingredients are moistened. Divide dough into three equal portions, shaping each portion into a ball.

Place each ball on a lightly greased baking sheet. Roll each into a 9-inch circle ¼-inch thick; trim edges, and prick with a fork. Bake at 450° for 10 minutes or until lightly browned. Cool on baking sheets 5 minutes; carefully transfer to wire racks to complete cooling.

Beat whipping cream until foamy. Gradually add powdered sugar, beating until soft peaks form.

Place 1 shortcake layer on serving plate. Arrange one-third of halved strawberries on layer, and spoon one-third of whipped cream over strawberries. Repeat procedure with remaining shortcakes, strawberries, and whipped cream. Garnish top of cake with whole strawberries. Yield: 12 servings.

Strawberry Shortcake is a towering confection of berries, pastry, and cream.

GREEK EASTER DINNER

"Christos anesti...Christ is risen!" cries a Greek child to start the Easter game, and "Aliothos anesti...truly Christ is risen," replies another. Then each, with a brightly dyed red egg in his hand, tries to crack the egg of his adversary. The game continues until the child with the last unbroken egg is declared the winner.

Greek communities in the South trace their beginnings back to the early 1900s. Among the oldest of these are in Norfolk, Virginia, and Tarpon Springs, Florida.

EASTER SOUP WITH EGG-LEMON SAUCE
ROAST LEG OF LAMB WITH POTATOES
STEWED GREEN BEANS * RICE PILAF
GREEK SALAD
PASTICHIO
GREEK SWEET BREAD
KARETHOPETA (Walnut Cake)

Serves 12

EASTER SOUP WITH EGG-LEMON SAUCE

1 lamb liver
1 lamb brain
1 lamb tongue
1 teaspoon salt
7 cups water
5 green onions, chopped
¼ cup plus 2 tablespoons butter or margarine
¼ teaspoon dillweed
¼ teaspoon pepper
½ cup uncooked regular rice
Egg-Lemon Sauce

Combine liver, brain, tongue, salt, and water in a large Dutch oven. Bring to a boil; cover and simmer 30 minutes or until meat is fork tender. Remove meat from broth. Cool; chop and set aside. Strain broth and set aside.

Sauté onion in butter in a heavy skillet until tender. Add chopped meat, dillweed, and pepper; cover and simmer 5 minutes. Add onion-meat mixture to reserved broth; cover and simmer 30 minutes. Add rice, and simmer an additional 20 minutes. Gently stir Egg-Lemon Sauce into simmering soup. (Maintain simmering temperature; do not increase heat.) Serve immediately. Yield: twelve ½-cup servings.

Egg-Lemon Sauce:

3 eggs, beaten
3 tablespoons lemon juice
3 tablespoons water
2 tablespoons all-purpose flour
1 cup chicken broth

Combine eggs, lemon juice, water, and flour in a small saucepan; beat until well blended. Cook over low heat 1 minute, stirring constantly. Gradually add chicken broth; cook over medium heat, stirring constantly, until thickened and bubbly. Yield: about 2½ cups.

Lilies, symbolic of Easter.

A Happy Eastertide

ROAST LEG OF LAMB WITH POTATOES

1 (5- to 7-pound) leg of lamb
2 cloves garlic, sliced
1¼ teaspoons salt
¾ teaspoon pepper
2 teaspoons dried whole oregano
3 cups water, divided
6 large potatoes, peeled and quartered
2 tablespoons lemon juice

Remove the fell (tissue-like covering) from lamb with a sharp knife. Make several small slits on outside of lamb, and stuff with garlic slices. Sprinkle with salt, pepper, and oregano.

Place lamb, fat side up, in a large roasting pan. Insert meat thermometer, being careful not to touch bone or fat. Add 1 cup water to roasting pan; bake at 350° for 30 minutes or until top of lamb is brown. Add 1 cup water to roasting pan; bake an additional 30 minutes.

Add remaining 1 cup water to roasting pan; arrange potatoes around lamb. Baste potatoes with pan drippings, and sprinkle lamb with lemon juice. Bake 2 hours or until meat thermometer registers 175°. Remove lamb and potatoes to a serving platter. Yield: 12 servings.

RICE PILAF

4½ cups chicken broth
1 cup plus 2 tablespoons
   butter or margarine
2¼ cups uncooked regular
   rice
1½ teaspoons chopped fresh
   parsley
½ teaspoon pepper

Combine broth and butter in
a large saucepan; bring to a boil.
Stir in rice, parsley, and pepper.
Reduce heat; cover and simmer
25 minutes or until all liquid is
absorbed. Yield: 12 servings.

GREEK SALAD

1 head iceberg lettuce, torn
4 to 5 leaves chicory, torn
4 to 5 leaves escarole, torn
4 to 5 leaves romaine, torn
4 to 5 leaves endive, torn
2 large tomatoes, peeled and
   cut into wedges
1 small green pepper, sliced
   into rings
1 Bermuda or red onion,
   thinly sliced and separated
   into rings
4 radishes, sliced
⅓ cup pitted ripe olives,
   drained
¼ cup crumbled feta cheese
9 Salonika Greek peppers
1 teaspoon dried whole
   oregano
¼ teaspoon salt
¼ teaspoon pepper
¾ cup olive oil
1 clove garlic, minced
¼ cup red wine vinegar

Combine first 9 ingredients in
a large salad bowl. Garnish with
ripe olives, feta cheese, and
Greek peppers.
Combine oregano, salt, pepper, oil, garlic, and vinegar in a
jar. Cover tightly, and shake
well. Pour over salad just before
serving, and toss lightly. Yield:
12 servings.

*Greek Easter Feast: Roast Leg of Lamb
with Potatoes, Greek Salad, Rice Pilaf.
Basket of red Easter eggs.*

STEWED GREEN BEANS

3½ pounds fresh green
   beans
3 large onions,
   chopped
½ cup plus 1 tablespoon
   olive oil
2¼ cups water
2½ tablespoons chopped
   fresh parsley
2¼ teaspoons salt
1 teaspoon pepper

Remove strings from beans.
Wash and cut beans into 1½-
inch pieces; drain.
Sauté onion in oil in a large
Dutch oven 5 minutes. Add
beans; sauté 8 minutes.
Add remaining ingredients;
bring mixture to a boil. Reduce
heat; cover and simmer 30 minutes or until beans are tender.
Yield: 12 servings.

PASTICHIO

1 (12-ounce) package elbow
  macaroni
1½ pounds ground beef
1 cup butter or margarine,
  divided
2 medium onions, chopped
½ cup chopped green
  pepper
1½ teaspoons salt
½ teaspoon pepper
1½ teaspoons dried whole
  oregano
½ (6-ounce) can tomato
  paste
½ cup water
1¾ cups grated Romano
  cheese, divided
Dash of ground cinnamon
2 egg whites, divided
1 quart milk
3 egg yolks
3 whole eggs
¾ cup plus 2 tablespoons
  all-purpose flour

Cook macaroni according to
package directions; drain well,
and set aside.

Brown beef in a large skillet,
stirring to crumble. Drain off
drippings; discard. Add ¼ cup
butter, onion, and green pepper; cook, stirring often, until
vegetables are tender. Add salt,
pepper, and oregano.

Combine tomato paste and
water; add to meat mixture.
Simmer, stirring occasionally,
until thickened. Remove from
heat. Stir in ½ cup cheese and
cinnamon. Beat 1 egg white (at
room temperature) until soft
peaks form. Add to meat mixture, blending well; set aside.

Scald milk in a large saucepan; set aside. Melt ½ cup butter in a heavy saucepan over low
heat; add flour, stirring until
smooth. Cook 1 minute, stirring constantly. Gradually add
milk, stirring constantly, until
thickened and bubbly. Remove

from heat. Add ¾ cup cheese;
stir until cheese melts.

Combine 3 egg yolks and 3
whole eggs in a large mixing
bowl; beat well. Gradually stir in
hot cream sauce mixture, stirring constantly; set aside.

Spread two-thirds of macaroni in a greased 12- x 8- x 2-
inch baking dish. Add remaining egg white; mix thoroughly.
Sprinkle ¼ cup cheese on top of
macaroni. Melt remaining ¼
cup butter; pour over cheese.
Spread meat mixture evenly
over surface. Cover with remaining macaroni; sprinkle
with remaining ¼ cup cheese.
Pour cream sauce over top. Bake
at 350° for 1 hour. Yield: 12
servings.

GREEK SWEET BREAD

1 cup milk, scalded
2 packages dry yeast
9½ cups all-purpose flour,
  divided
6 eggs, beaten
1 cup butter or margarine,
  melted
1½ cups sugar
1 cup warm milk (105°
  to 115°)
1 tablespoon salt
2 teaspoons vanilla extract
1 teaspoon grated orange rind
2 egg yolks, beaten

Allow 1 cup scalded milk to
cool to 105° to 115°. Combine
cooled milk, yeast, and 1 cup
flour in a bowl; cover and let
stand in a warm place (85°), free
from drafts, overnight.

Combine beaten eggs, butter,
sugar, 1 cup warm milk, salt,
vanilla, and orange rind in a
large mixing bowl; mix well. Add
yeast mixture; stir well. Gradually add remaining 8½ cups
flour to make a soft dough.

Turn dough out onto a floured
surface, and knead 8 minutes or
until smooth and elastic. Place
dough in a well-greased bowl,
turning to grease top. Cover and
repeat rising procedure 1 hour
and 45 minutes or until doubled
in bulk.

Punch dough down; cover and

repeat rising procedure 1 hour
or until doubled in bulk. Punch
dough down; turn out onto a
floured surface.

Divide dough into 6 portions;
shape each into a 22-inch rope.
Pinch 2 ropes together at one
end to seal. Twist ropes together. Shape twist into a ring,
and place on a greased baking
sheet. Repeat procedure with remaining ropes.

Cover ropes, and repeat rising
procedure 1 hour or until doubled in bulk.

Gently brush loaves with
beaten egg yolks. Bake at 350°
for 20 minutes. Cover loaves
loosely with aluminum foil; continue to bake at 350° for 20 minutes or until loaves sound
hollow when tapped. Transfer
loaves to wire racks to cool.
Yield: 3 loaves.

KARETHOPETA

6 eggs
2 cups sugar, divided
2 cups chopped walnuts
1 (6-ounce) package zwieback
  toast slices, finely crushed
2 teaspoons baking powder
½ teaspoon ground cinnamon
½ teaspoon salt
2 teaspoons vanilla extract
1 cup water
½ cup whipping cream,
  whipped (optional)

Combine eggs and 1 cup
sugar; beat well.

Combine walnuts, zwieback,
baking powder, cinnamon, and
salt in a medium mixing bowl;
add egg mixture, stirring well.
Add vanilla, and mix well.

Pour batter into a greased and
floured 8-inch square baking
pan. Bake at 325° for 40 minutes or until a wooden pick inserted in center comes out
clean. Cool completely in pan.

Combine remaining 1 cup
sugar and water in a small
saucepan. Bring to a boil; reduce heat, and simmer, uncovered, 10 minutes. Pour hot
syrup over cooled cake. Cut into
squares, and serve with
whipped cream, if desired.
Yield: 16 servings.

MEMPHIS PASSOVER

A Seder dinner in the South, such as this one from Memphis, may vary somewhat from its Northern counterpart. The traditional lamb has been hard to find; beef brisket or fowl is frequently eaten instead. And it has been noted that more guests are invited than in other parts of the country.

The Seder dinner, Feast of the Passover, is a family service of great symbolic beauty. Relatives and guests are included; it is a time of reunion. Unleavened bread is eaten in memory of the haste of the Jews' exodus. No wheat flour is used; matzo meal and potato flour only are allowed. Seder means order and stands for the ritual of the feast.

GEFILTE FISH
CHICKEN SOUP WITH MATZO BALLS
CRANBERRY BAKED CHICKEN BREASTS
CARROT TZIMMES
MATZO FRUIT KUGEL
STEAMED BROCCOLI
LEMON CURD TRIFLE

Serves 12

GEFILTE FISH

6 pounds buffalo fish
1 large onion, sliced
2 stalks celery, sliced
2 carrots, sliced
2 tablespoons salt, divided
1 teaspoon sugar
4 quarts water
6 eggs
3 stalks celery, finely chopped
2 onions, finely chopped
1 carrot, finely chopped
¼ cup plus 2 tablespoons matzo meal
½ teaspoon pepper
Red horseradish
Carrot strips (optional)
Chopped fresh parsley (optional)

Fillet fish; set aside. Wrap bones securely in cheese cloth; place in an 8½-quart stock pot. Add sliced onion, celery, carrots, 1 tablespoon salt, sugar, and water. Bring to a boil; cover and simmer 30 minutes. Strain liquid; discard vegetables and bones. Allow liquid to return to a simmer.

Grind fish; combine fish, eggs, chopped celery, onion, carrot, matzo meal, remaining salt, and pepper in a large mixing bowl; mix well. Shape fish mixture into oblong patties using ½ cup mixture per patty. Drop patties into simmering liquid; cover and cook over low heat 3 hours. Let gefilte fish cool completely in cooking liquid; chill thoroughly. Serve with red horseradish, and garnish with carrot strips and parsley, if desired. Yield: about 3 dozen.

CHICKEN SOUP WITH MATZO BALLS

1 (5-pound) baking hen, quartered
4 quarts water
4 stalks celery, cut into 3-inch pieces
4 carrots, cut into 3-inch pieces
1 large onion, quartered
1 small green pepper, seeded and coarsely chopped
1 bay leaf
1 tablespoon salt
Matzo Balls

Combine all ingredients except Matzo Balls in a large Dutch oven; bring to a boil. Reduce heat; cover and simmer 3 hours or until hen is tender.

Remove hen from broth, and reserve for use in another recipe. Strain broth, and discard vegetables.

Return broth to Dutch oven; bring to a boil. Drop Matzo Balls into broth. Cover and cook 30 to 40 minutes. Yield: 12 servings.

Matzo Balls:

4 eggs, slightly beaten
¼ cup rendered chicken fat
¼ cup water
1½ teaspoons salt
1 cup matzo meal

Combine eggs, chicken fat, water, and salt in a medium mixing bowl; beat well. Stir in matzo meal. Cover and refrigerate at least 2 hours. Shape dough into 1½-inch balls. Yield: 16 matzo balls.

Elements of a traditional Seder dinner: Gefilte Fish, Matzo Ball Soup, and symbolic Seder Plate.

CARROT TZIMMES

CRANBERRY BAKED CHICKEN BREASTS

2 medium onions, chopped
2 cloves garlic, minced
1 tablespoon butter or margarine, melted
1 (16-ounce) can jellied cranberry sauce
1 (8-ounce) bottle commercial French salad dressing
6 whole chicken breasts, split

Sauté onion and garlic in butter in a heavy saucepan until onion is tender. Combine cranberry sauce, dressing, and sautéed vegetables in a large mixing bowl; stir well.

Place chicken breast halves in a well-greased 13- x 9- x 2-inch baking dish. Pour sauce over chicken. Bake, uncovered, at 400° for 1 hour and 20 minutes or until sauce is bubbly. Yield: 12 servings.

4 to 5 pounds boneless beef short ribs, trimmed
2 medium onions, sliced
6 stalks celery
2 teaspoons salt
1 teaspoon pepper
1 gallon water
10 medium carrots, cut into ¼-inch slices
½ cup honey
¼ cup powdered potato starch
Potato Kugel

Combine beef, onion, celery, salt, pepper, and water in large stock pot; bring to a boil. Cover; reduce heat, and simmer 1½ hours or until meat is slightly tender. Remove meat from broth and cut into serving-size pieces. Strain broth; discard vegetables, and reserve 1½ quarts broth.

Combine meat, carrots, honey, and potato starch. Divide mixture evenly in 2 greased 12- x 7½- x 1½-inch baking dishes. Pour 2 cups of reserved

broth over each casserole. Bake, uncovered, at 350° for 1 hour. Pour an additional 1 cup of remaining reserved broth over each casserole; continue baking 30 minutes.

Drop Potato Kugel mixture by heaping teaspoonfuls at 1-inch intervals onto casseroles. Bake, uncovered, an additional hour or until potatoes are lightly browned. Yield: 12 servings.

Potato Kugel:

3 large potatoes, peeled and grated
1 large onion, grated
1 egg, beaten
1½ tablespoons rendered chicken fat
½ teaspoon salt
⅛ teaspoon pepper

Combine potatoes, onion, egg, chicken fat, salt, and pepper; mixing well. Yield: about 2½ cups.

MATZO FRUIT KUGEL

6 matzos
6 eggs, well beaten
2 large apples, unpeeled, cored, and grated
1 (17-ounce) can apricot halves, drained
1 (15¼-ounce) can pineapple tidbits, undrained
¾ cup golden raisins
¼ cup plus 1 tablespoon sugar, divided
Grated rind of 1 lemon
1 tablespoon lemon juice
1½ teaspoons ground cinnamon, divided
2 tablespoons butter or margarine, melted
1 tablespoon butter or margarine, softened
2 tablespoons red currant jelly

Crumble matzos into a large mixing bowl; cover with water. Soak 2 minutes; drain well.

Combine eggs, apple, apricot halves, pineapple, raisins, 3 tablespoons sugar, lemon rind, juice, and 1 teaspoon cinnamon in a large mixing bowl; stir well. Add matzos and 2 tablespoons melted butter, stirring well.

Grease a 13- x 9- x 2-inch baking dish with remaining butter. Spoon fruit mixture into prepared dish.

Combine remaining 2 tablespoons sugar and ½ teaspoon cinnamon; mix well. Sprinkle sugar mixture evenly over fruit mixture, and dot with currant jelly. Bake at 325° for 45 minutes or until golden brown. Yield: 12 servings.

STEAMED BROCCOLI

3 pounds fresh broccoli
¼ cup lemon juice

Trim off large leaves of broccoli, and remove tough ends of lower stalks. Wash broccoli thoroughly, and separate into spears. Arrange in steaming rack with stalks to center of rack. Place over boiling water; cover and steam 15 minutes.

Sprinkle with lemon juice before serving. Yield: 12 servings.

LEMON CURD TRIFLE

10 eggs, separated
1¾ cups sugar, divided
¾ cup powdered potato starch
¼ cup matzo cake meal
1 tablespoon grated orange rind
1 teaspoon grated lemon rind
3 tablespoons orange juice
1 tablespoon lemon juice
Lemon Curd
1 quart fresh strawberries, hulled and sliced
Whole strawberries
Whipped cream

Beat egg whites (at room temperature) in a large mixing bowl until foamy. Gradually add 1 cup sugar, 2 tablespoons at a time, beating 5 minutes or until stiff peaks form. Set side.

Place egg yolks in a large mixing bowl; beat at high speed of electric mixer 6 minutes or until thick and lemon colored. Gradually add remaining sugar, beating constantly until thoroughly blended.

Combine potato starch and cake meal. Set aside.

Combine orange and lemon rinds and juices. Add to egg yolk mixture alternately with potato starch mixture, beginning and ending with dry mixture. Gently fold in egg white mixture.

Pour batter into an ungreased 10-inch tube pan, spreading evenly with a spatula. Bake at 325° for 1 hour and 20 minutes or until cake springs back when lightly touched. Remove from oven; invert pan, and cool completely (about 40 minutes) before removing from pan.

Slice cake; line bottom and sides of a 3-quart serving bowl with slices. Pour half of Lemon Curd over cake. Top with sliced strawberries. Spoon remaining Lemon Curd over strawberries. Garnish with whole strawberries and whipped cream. Yield: 12 servings.

Lemon Curd:

6 eggs
2 egg yolks
2 cups sugar
¼ cup grated lemon rind
¾ cup lemon juice
1 cup butter or margarine

Combine eggs, yolks, and sugar in top of a double boiler, stirring well. Add remaining ingredients; place over gently boiling water. Cook, stirring constantly, until smooth and thickened. Remove from heat; let cool. Chill. Yield: 4 cups.

Family and friends prepare to celebrate Passover.

Courtesy of Lewis Schmier

Spring Rites

A spring garden radiates with color in Durham, North Carolina.

The flowering gardens of the South furnish a visual feast to people who travel from all parts of the country to savor their splendor. Traveling the temperate rain forest country, tourists can follow the blossoming of trees, shrubs, and flower gardens. From the warm Gulf waters northward, nature shows a riotous progression of color from azaleas to flowering dogwoods, all the blossoming things that vary from one state to the next.

The English have always loved their gardens; it was natural for the settlers to establish them in their new habitat. The formal gardens around Williamsburg and the James River country still enchant the eye. Herb gardening, too, is well represented in the tours available, serving as classrooms for herbalists.

Countless garden clubs have expended their energies in the beautification of Southern towns and cities, and the fame of their projects has spread. Two sterling examples follow, and illustrate again how, in the South, good food is hand in glove with all good times. For fun, note the origin of the "Queen" luncheon in Natchez, Mississippi, and try a different creamed chicken dish. Or if you crave crabcakes with your sightseeing, Maryland is the place to go.

NATCHEZ PILGRIMAGE QUEEN LUNCHEON

There is a women's group in Natchez that probably has more fun than the law allows. It is the Society for the Preservation and Maintenance of Aged Monarchs — every member a past queen of the Natchez Garden Club Pilgrimage. Their first luncheon was in 1952, the year Katherine Blankenstein, nee Boatner, was queen.

The following year, Katherine designed the club's coat of arms with cane, crutch, crown. . .and cocktail glass. And she made the doll that became their symbol and still presides over the annual gathering. The food is exquisite, as one would expect; think of creamed chicken over avocado dressing! The ambience is one of "foolishness, lots of fun." To appreciate their marching song, remember to sing it to the tune of "Just a Song at Twilight," and make it slow, sad, and shaky, but stirring.

MARTINIS * BLOODY MARYS
AVOCADO DRESSING WITH CREAMED CHICKEN
BUTTERED GREEN BEANS
TOASTED BISCUITS WITH OLIVE SPREAD
PEPPERED FRUIT
LEMON PIE

Serves 12

MARTINI

⅔ cup gin
2½ tablespoons dry white
  vermouth
Finely crushed ice
1 pimiento-stuffed olive

Combine gin and vermouth; pour mixture over ice, and stir well. Strain into glass. Garnish with a pimiento-stuffed olive. Yield: 1 serving.

BLOODY MARY

½ cup tomato juice
2 tablespoons beef broth
1 tablespoon spicy-hot
  vegetable juice
½ teaspoon Worcestershire
  sauce
½ teaspoon lemon juice
½ teaspoon lime juice
Dash of celery salt
⅛ teaspoon steak sauce
¼ cup vodka
Crushed ice

Combine first 8 ingredients; mix well. Cover and chill thoroughly. Stir in vodka just before serving. Serve over crushed ice. Yield: 1 serving.

AVOCADO DRESSING
WITH CREAMED CHICKEN

5 cups cornbread crumbs
3 cups soft bread cubes
½ teaspoon salt
1 teaspoon pepper
1 teaspoon dried whole thyme
1 cup chopped celery
1 cup sliced fresh
  mushrooms
1 cup chopped onion
½ cup chopped green onion
¼ cup plus 2 tablespoons
  butter or margarine
2 ripe avocados, peeled and
  cubed
1 cup chopped pecans
⅓ cup chopped fresh parsley
4 eggs, beaten
4 cups chicken broth
Creamed Chicken

Combine cornbread crumbs, bread cubes, salt, pepper, and thyme in a large bowl.

Sauté celery, mushrooms, and onion in butter until tender; add to cornbread mixture, stirring well. Stir in next 5 ingredients.

Spoon dressing into a lightly greased 13- x 9- x 2-inch baking pan. Bake at 375° for 1 hour or until browned. Cut into squares, and spoon on Creamed Chicken. Yield: 12 servings.

Creamed Chicken:

¼ cup butter or margarine
½ cup all-purpose flour
3 cups chicken broth
2½ cups cubed cooked
  chicken
¼ cup chopped fresh parsley

Melt butter in a heavy saucepan over low heat; add flour, and stir until smooth. Cook 1 minute, stirring constantly. Gradually add broth; cook over medium heat, stirring constantly, until thickened and bubbly. Stir in chicken and parsley. Yield: 4½ cups.

BUTTERED GREEN BEANS

3 pounds fresh green
beans
5 cups water
1 (½-pound) ham hock
2 teaspoons sugar
1 teaspoon salt
½ teaspoon pepper
¼ cup butter or margarine

Remove strings from beans.
Cut beans into 1½-inch pieces,
and wash.

Place water and ham hock in a
large Dutch oven; bring to a
boil. Reduce heat; cover and
simmer 1 hour. Add beans,
sugar, salt, and pepper; cook 50
minutes or until beans are
tender. Remove from heat;
drain and add butter. Cover and
let stand 5 minutes or until butter is melted. Toss beans well
before serving. Yield: 10 to 12
servings.

TOASTED BISCUITS WITH OLIVE SPREAD

2 cups (8 ounces) shredded
sharp Cheddar cheese
1 (4½-ounce) can chopped
ripe olives, drained
2 teaspoons finely chopped
onion
⅛ teaspoon curry powder
¼ cup mayonnaise
12 (2-inch) biscuits, baked

Combine cheese, olives,
onion, curry powder, and
mayonnaise; stir well.

Split biscuits; spread cheese
mixture evenly over each half,
and place on ungreased baking
sheets. Bake at 350° for 10 minutes or until bubbly. Serve hot.
Yield: 2 dozen.

PEPPERED FRUIT

2 apples, unpeeled and
coarsely chopped
2 cucumbers, peeled and
sliced
2 cantaloupes, peeled and
thinly sliced
½ cup chopped fresh parsley
2 tablespoons lemon juice
1 cup vegetable oil
¼ cup plus 2 tablespoons
lemon juice
1½ teaspoons Dijon
mustard
1 teaspoon coarsely ground
black pepper
¾ teaspoon salt
½ teaspoon dried whole
tarragon
Lettuce leaves

Combine apples, cucumbers,
cantaloupe, and parsley in a
large bowl; toss lightly with 2 tablespoons lemon juice.

Combine remaining ingre-
dients, except lettuce leaves, in
a jar. Cover tightly, and shake
vigorously; pour dressing over
fruit. Cover and chill at least 2
hours. Serve on lettuce leaves.
Yield: 12 servings.

LEMON PIE

2 cups sugar
¼ cup plus 2 tablespoons
cornstarch
½ cup butter or margarine,
softened
2 tablespoons grated lemon
rind
¼ cup plus 2 tablespoons
lemon juice
6 egg yolks, beaten
2 cups milk
2 (8-ounce) cartons
commercial sour cream
2 baked 8-inch pastry shells
Whipped cream (optional)
Chocolate curls (optional)

Combine sugar and corn-
starch in a large, heavy saucepan; mix well. Add butter,
lemon rind, juice, and egg yolks;
stir well. Gradually add milk,
stirring constantly. Cook over
low heat, stirring constantly,
until mixture is thickened. Remove from heat; chill 1 hour.

Fold in sour cream, and pour
filling into pastry shells. Chill 4
hours. Garnish with whipped
cream and chocolate curls, if desired. Yield: two 8-inch pies.

Aged Monarchs annual luncheon: 1953 doll presides.

MARYLAND
GARDEN PILGRIMAGE LUNCHEON

Back in 1930, the Federated Garden Clubs of Maryland organized the first House and Garden Pilgrimage, opening private homes and gardens as a benefit to finance the reconstruction of the garden house of Stratford, Robert E. Lee's Virginia birthplace. Today visitors come from all over the country to participate in the Pilgrimage.

Different communities play host to the Pilgrimage from year to year, the local Garden Club taking charge of the luncheon. Depend on it; the menu is superbly regional, with crabmeat and Maryland ham. Luncheons are usually served in churches, and some menus haven't changed over the years. Why change a successful formula?

Many notable restorations behind them, the Federation now concentrates on supporting Annapolis' historic Hammond-Harwood House.

OLD DURHAM CHURCH CRAB CAKES
THIN SLICES OF COUNTRY HAM
GREEN PEAS WITH SPRING ONIONS
COLD SLAW
JUBILEE ROLLS
MARYLAND FUDGE CAKE
GLAZED STRAWBERRY TARTS

Serves 8 to 10

OLD DURHAM CHURCH CRAB CAKES

2 pounds fresh crabmeat, drained and flaked
2 cups soft breadcrumbs
2 eggs, beaten
¼ cup mayonnaise
2 tablespoons minced onion
2 teaspoons lemon juice
2 dashes hot sauce
2 teaspoons salt
1 teaspoon dry mustard
¼ teaspoon paprika
¼ teaspoon pepper
3 tablespoons vegetable oil

Combine all ingredients, except oil, mixing well; shape into 2½-inch patties. Cover and chill at least 1 hour.

Heat oil in a large skillet; cook patties over medium heat 8 minutes on each side or until golden brown. Drain on paper towels; serve immediately. Yield: about 2 dozen.

GREEN PEAS WITH SPRING ONIONS

Lettuce leaves
2 (10-ounce) packages frozen English peas
2 dozen green onion bulbs, cut into ¼-inch pieces
¼ cup plus 2 tablespoons butter or margarine
1 teaspoon salt

Line a small Dutch oven with lettuce leaves. Add peas, onion bulbs, butter, and salt. Top with lettuce leaves. Cover and cook over low heat 15 minutes or until peas are tender. Remove lettuce leaves; discard. Place peas and onions in a serving bowl. Yield: 8 to 10 servings.

COLD SLAW

8 cups finely sliced cabbage
1 tablespoon finely chopped celery
2 eggs, beaten
2 tablespoons sugar
1 teaspoon dry mustard
½ teaspoon salt
¼ teaspoon pepper
2 tablespoons butter or margarine, softened
½ cup vinegar
½ cup whipping cream

Combine cabbage and celery; set aside.

Place eggs and sugar in a medium saucepan; beat well. Combine mustard, salt, and pepper; add to egg mixture. Add butter, and slowly stir in vinegar. Cook over low heat, stirring constantly, until mixture is thickened. Remove from heat; chill.

Add whipping cream to chilled mixture, stirring well. Pour sauce over cabbage mixture; toss well. Cover and chill. Yield: 8 to 10 servings.

JUBILEE ROLLS

¾ cup boiling water
¼ cup plus 2 tablespoons
    shortening
¼ cup sugar
½ package dry yeast
½ teaspoon sugar
2 tablespoons warm water
    (105° to 115°)
1 egg, beaten
2½ cups all-purpose flour
1 teaspoon salt

Combine water, shortening, and ¼ cup sugar; stir until shortening melts. Cool to lukewarm (105° to 115°).

Dissolve yeast and ½ teaspoon sugar in 2 tablespoons warm water; stir well. Let yeast mixture stand 5 minutes or until bubbly. Add yeast mixture to shortening mixture, stirring well. Stir in egg.

Combine flour and salt, stirring well. Gradually add flour mixture to yeast mixture, beating well. Cover; refrigerate at least 2 hours or overnight.

Punch dough down. Let rest 5 minutes. Heavily grease miniature muffin pans. Shape dough into 1-inch balls; place one ball in each muffin cup. Cover and let rise in a warm place (85°), free from drafts, 35 minutes or until doubled in bulk. Bake at 350° for 10 minutes or until golden brown. Yield: 3 dozen.

A typical Garden Pilgrimage luncheon served in Maryland will usually feature country ham and crab as well as a dessert choice.

MARYLAND FUDGE CAKE

½ cup butter or margarine,
    softened
1 cup sugar
2 eggs
2 (1-ounce) squares
    unsweetened chocolate
½ cup all-purpose flour
½ teaspoon salt
1 teaspoon vanilla extract
1 cup chopped black walnuts
    or pecans
Frosting (recipe follows)

Cream butter in a large mixing bowl; gradually add sugar, beating well. Add eggs; beat well. Set aside.

Place chocolate in top of a double boiler; bring water to a boil. Reduce heat to low, and cook until chocolate melts; let cool slightly.

Sift together flour and salt. Add flour mixture and chocolate to creamed mixture; mix well. Stir in vanilla and walnuts.

Pour batter into a waxed paper-lined and greased 8-inch square baking pan. Bake at 400° for 20 minutes or until a wooden pick inserted in center comes out clean. Cool in pan on a wire rack. Frost and cut into 2-inch squares to serve. Yield: one 8-inch cake.

Frosting:

2 teaspoons butter or
    margarine, softened
2 cups sifted powdered sugar
3 tablespoons cocoa
3 tablespoons hot coffee

Cream butter; gradually add sugar, beating well. Add cocoa and coffee; beat until smooth. Yield: enough frosting for an 8-inch cake.

GLAZED STRAWBERRY TARTS

½ cup sugar
1 tablespoon cornstarch
½ cup water
2 tablespoons strawberry-
    flavored gelatin
1 pint fresh strawberries,
    washed and hulled
8 (3-inch) baked tart shells

Combine sugar and cornstarch in a saucepan; stir in water. Cook over medium heat, stirring constantly, until thickened and clear. Remove from heat; add gelatin, stirring until dissolved.

Place 3 to 4 strawberries in each tart shell. Spoon 3 tablespoons glaze into each shell. Refrigerate tarts before serving. Yield: 8 servings.

Hats vie with wares at Baltimore Flower Mart, 1910.

Maryland Historical Society

May Day

Folklorists are unanimous in disagreeing over the origins of May Day celebrations. Link May Day, if you wish, to the Roman festival of Flora, goddess of flowers, which began about 238 B.C. Or assume that Romulus started it right after the founding of Rome. Or settle for a man named Servilius, who, by order of the Senate, arranged for its celebration in 173 B.C. It probably had its roots in old India and Egypt anyway, when it would have coincided with the Spring fertility rites.

What is certain is that the Romans brought the May Day celebration to Britain, and it became a yearly highlight in medieval and Tudor England. Everyone was up at dawn to "go a-Maying," gathering hawthorn branches, playing on horns and tabors, and singing. The Maypole, usually birch, was brought in by oxen, set up in the village, and decorated with flowers, ribbons, and garlands.

Of the merriment, this by poet Robert Herrick:

> Can such delights be in the streets,
>
> And open fields, and we not see it?. . .
>
> But, my Corinna, come, let's go a-Maying.

Enter the Puritans, sworn enemies of fun and games. The Maypole was denounced as an eyesore, "a stynking idea," about which people leaped and danced like heathens. "Sin now appears with a brazen face," wrote an objector. They lobbied Parliament into banning Maypoles in 1644, but when the Stuarts replaced the ruling Tudors, the Maypole returned too.

Invitation to a children's May Ball, dated 1909.

The Historic New Orleans Collection, 533 Royal Street

PICNIC IN MAY

In a 1916 directive to Virginia Public Schools from the Department of Public Instruction, some guidelines were given for the May Day celebration: "If at all possible, make it a picnic occasion. By some simple contest in advance select a May Queen."

The program itself was outlined in detail and included some procedures that remained standard for May Day observances for decades. There are people yet living who remember singing "Welcome Sweet Springtime," the recitations by nerve-wracked, crepe paper-clad children, and the interminable speech by a native son.

VIRGINIA HAM SALAD
GINGER CREAM TRIANGLES
PIMIENTO CHEESE STUFFED CELERY
VIRGINIA BUTTERMILK BISCUITS
STRAWBERRIES IN RIBBON BEDECKED BASKETS
SPRINGTIME PUNCH
CHOCOLATE GEMS

Serves 12

VIRGINIA HAM SALAD

2 cups diced cooked ham
1 cup diced celery
1 cup sweet pickle relish
4 hard-cooked eggs, finely chopped
¼ cup plus 2 tablespoons mayonnaise
1 teaspoon prepared mustard
12 medium tomatoes
1½ teaspoons salt
Lettuce leaves

Combine ham, celery, pickle relish, eggs, mayonnaise, and mustard; mix well. Chill.

Cut tops from tomatoes; scoop out pulp, leaving shells intact. Sprinkle inside of each tomato with ⅛ teaspoon salt, Invert on paper towels; drain.

Spoon ham salad into tomato shells. Serve on lettuce leaves. Yield: 12 servings.

GINGER CREAM TRIANGLES

1 (8-ounce) package cream cheese, softened
¼ cup mayonnaise
⅔ cup chopped pecans
1 teaspoon ground ginger
24 slices thin-sliced whole wheat bread

Beat cream cheese and mayonnaise at medium speed of electric mixer until smooth and fluffy. Stir in pecans and ginger, distributing evenly.

Remove crust from bread. Spread cream cheese mixture evenly over 12 slices of bread. Place remaining bread slices over cream cheese mixture to make sandwiches. Cut each sandwich into 4 triangles. Yield: 4 dozen appetizer sandwiches or 2 dozen whole sandwiches.

PIMIENTO CHEESE STUFFED CELERY

2 cups (8 ounces) shredded sharp Cheddar cheese
2 cups (8 ounces) shredded mild Cheddar cheese
1 (2-ounce) jar chopped pimiento, drained
¾ cup cottage cheese
½ to ¾ cup mayonnaise
8 to 10 drops hot sauce
Pinch of salt
¼ teaspoon pepper
4 stalks celery
Paprika

Position knife blade in food processor bowl; add Cheddar cheese and pimiento. Process 3 to 5 seconds. Stop processor, and scrape sides of bowl with a rubber spatula.

Add next five ingredients; process until smooth. Add additional mayonnaise, if necessary. Chill. Wash celery, and cut into 3-inch pieces. Using a pastry bag, pipe cheese mixture into celery pieces; sprinkle with paprika. Yield: 12 servings.

Note: If food processor is not available, combine ingredients in a bowl; beat with electric mixer until smooth.

VIRGINIA BUTTERMILK BISCUITS

2 cups all-purpose flour, sifted
1 tablespoon baking powder
¼ teaspoon baking soda
½ teaspoon salt
¼ cup shortening
¾ cup buttermilk
2 tablespoons butter or margarine, melted

Combine flour, baking powder, soda, and salt; stir well. Cut in shortening until mixture resembles coarse meal. Sprinkle buttermilk evenly over flour mixture; stir until dry ingredients are moistened.

Turn dough out onto a lightly floured surface; knead 10 to 12 times. Roll dough to ½-inch thickness; cut with a 1¾-inch biscuit cutter. Place biscuits on ungreased baking sheets. Brush tops with melted butter. Bake at 450° for 8 minutes or until lightly browned. Yield: about 2 dozen.

1925 May Day dance, Louisville, looks quaint today.

SPRINGTIME PUNCH

3 quarts water
8 quart-size tea bags
1 cup sugar
1 (12-ounce) can frozen lemonade concentrate, thawed and undiluted
1 (32-ounce) bottle ginger ale, chilled

Bring water to a boil, and add tea bags. Remove from heat; cover and let stand 10 minutes. Discard tea bags; add sugar and lemonade concentrate, stirring until dissolved. Chill thoroughly. Stir in ginger ale before serving. Yield: about 1 gallon.

A May Day picnic should be pretty and spring-like, fit for the Queen of the May herself. Like this one, with a ribbon-bedecked basket of strawberries.

CHOCOLATE GEMS

½ cup butter or margarine, softened
1 cup sugar
2 eggs, separated
¼ cup boiling water
2 tablespoons cocoa
¼ teaspoon baking soda
1¼ cups all-purpose flour
2 teaspoons baking powder
Pinch of salt
1 teaspoon ground cinnamon
½ teaspoon ground nutmeg
½ cup milk
Glaze (recipe follows)

Cream butter; gradually add sugar, beating well. Add egg yolks, one at a time, beating well after each addition.

Combine boiling water and cocoa; stir until cocoa dissolves. Let stand 5 minutes. Stir in soda. Add cocoa mixture to creamed mixture, beating well.

Sift together flour, baking powder, salt, and spices; add to creamed mixture alternately with milk, beginning and ending with flour mixture. Beat egg whites (at room temperature) until stiff peaks form; fold into creamed mixture.

Spoon into well-greased muffin pans, filling half full. Bake at 350° for 15 to 20 minutes. Remove from muffin pans; spoon glaze over tops. Yield: 2 dozen.

Glaze:

2½ cups sifted powdered sugar
3 tablespoons milk
2 tablespoons butter or margarine, softened
2 teaspoons vanilla extract
1 teaspoon rum extract

Combine all ingredients in top of a double boiler, stirring well. Place over boiling water; cook until sugar is dissolved, stirring frequently. Remove from heat; beat until mixture is slightly thickened. Use immediately. Yield: about 1 cup.

MAY DAY BOX SUPPER

While the Puritans were able to dampen most of the merriment in the Northern colonies, they had very little to do with the shaping of May Day and other holiday celebrations in the South. Our English settlers brought along the custom of giving May baskets, with no apologies. Children made little baskets, sometimes of woven paper strips, filling them with flowers, verses, and candies to hang on friends' doorknobs. "May basket!" the child would call and run away.

Then, as customs are wont to do, May baskets went into eclipse. There has been a revival in recent years, however, and many children now make May baskets, not just for playmates and family, but also for lonely people and shut-ins.

MEAT TURNOVERS
BANANA-PEANUT SALAD
SWEET PICKLES * CARROT CURLS
CELERY STICKS * RADISH ROSES
MINT MARSHMALLOWS
PEANUT BRITTLE
COCONUT FUDGE
ASSORTED FRESH FRUITS

Serves 18

Lunch break at the May Day Pageant, Siloam, Georgia, 1941.

MEAT TURNOVERS

½ pound ground beef
2 small potatoes, peeled and
  cubed
1 small onion, finely chopped
½ teaspoon salt
¼ teaspoon pepper
¼ cup water
Pastry (recipe follows)
Catsup (optional)

Combine beef, potatoes,
onion, salt, and pepper in a
Dutch oven. Cook until beef is
browned, stirring to crumble;
drain well.

Roll pastry to ⅛-inch thickness on a lightly floured surface.
Cut twenty 4½-inch circles.
Spoon 1 tablespoon meat mixture on each pastry circle.
Sprinkle each pastry circle
evenly with about 1 teaspoon
water. Moisten edges of circles;
fold pastry in even halves. Using
a fork dipped in flour, press
edges together to seal.

Place on lightly greased baking sheets. Bake at 375° for 1
hour or until lightly browned.
Serve with catsup, if desired.
Yield: about 2 dozen.

Pastry:

5 cups all-purpose flour
2 teaspoons salt
1 cup plus 1½ teaspoons
  shortening
6 to 7 tablespoons cold water

Combine flour and salt; cut in
shortening with a pastry
blender until mixture resembles
coarse meal. With a fork, gradually stir in enough cold water to
moisten dry ingredients. Shape
pastry dough into a ball. Yield:
enough pastry for about 2 dozen
turnovers.

BANANA-PEANUT SALAD

1 cup mayonnaise
1 cup creamy peanut butter
6 medium bananas
3 cups unsalted, dry-roasted
  peanuts, finely chopped

Combine mayonnaise and
peanut butter; mix well.

Slice each banana into thirds,
and place each piece on a
wooden skewer. Coat banana
pieces with mayonnaise mixture. Roll banana pieces in
chopped peanuts, turning to
coat evenly.

Place banana pieces on a
waxed paper-lined baking sheet;
cover lightly, and freeze overnight. Yield: 18 servings.

MINT MARSHMALLOWS

2½ tablespoons butter or
  margarine, softened
1¾ cups sifted powdered
  sugar
1½ tablespoons milk
9 drops oil of peppermint
Red food coloring
1 (10-ounce) package large
  marshmallows

Cream butter; gradually add
sugar, beating well. Add milk
and oil of peppermint; beat until
spreading consistency. Tint
frosting with food coloring to
desired color.

Spread frosting on top and
sides of each marshmallow,
using the tines of a fork to sup-
port each marshmallow during
frosting procedure. Yield: about
3 dozen.

PEANUT BRITTLE

2 cups sugar
1 cup light corn syrup
2½ cups raw peanuts
½ teaspoon baking soda
1 teaspoon water
1 teaspoon vanilla extract

Combine sugar and syrup in a
Dutch oven; cook over low heat
until mixture reaches soft ball
stage (240°). Add peanuts; cook,
stirring constantly, until mixture reaches hard crack stage
(300°). Remove from heat; stir
in soda, water, and vanilla.

Spread mixture onto a warm,
buttered 15- x 10- x 1-inch jellyroll pan. Allow peanut brittle
to cool; break into pieces. Yield:
about 2 pounds.

*Homemade candies left
over from May baskets are
used for dessert in this
Box Supper menu.*

COCONUT FUDGE

2 cups sugar
1 cup whipping cream
2 tablespoons butter or
  margarine, melted
1 teaspoon vanilla extract
½ cup flaked coconut

Combine sugar, whipping
cream, butter, and vanilla in a
medium saucepan. Bring mixture to a boil. Reduce heat, and
cook, uncovered, until mixture
reaches thread stage (230°). Remove from heat, and let stand
15 minutes.

Beat mixture at medium
speed of electric mixer 2 to 3
minutes or until fudge is thick
and begins to lose its gloss.

Pour 1 tablespoon fudge into
paper-lined miniature muffin
pans. Sprinkle coconut evenly
over each piece, and refrigerate
8 hours or overnight. Yield:
about 3½ dozen.

Derby Day

The beautiful Oakland Race Track replaced Louisville Turf on the riverfront in 1832 and widened Louisville's reputation as a racing city. Oakland closed down in the depression of the 1850s and lay dormant until 1872, when Colonel Meriwether Lewis Clark went to England to study horse racing. What he brought back was the system of racing by class and age. His ideas resulted in the organization, in 1874, of the Louisville Jockey Club, which later became known as Churchill Downs.

The Downs was built on 100 acres purchased from Lewis' uncles, John and Henry Churchill. The race was for three-year-olds with $1,000 purse added, an unheard-of amount of money. Also unheard-of was the crowd of 10,000 in attendance at the race. Fifteen thoroughbreds were entered, and racing history was made when Aristides was ridden to victory by black jockey Oliver Lewis. Aristides set a new time record as well as a precedent that May 17, 1875. Racing's new capital was Churchill Downs.

There is a hint of madness in the air in Louisville as the first Saturday in May draws near, and natives are well into their second century of coping with it. They shrug it off as "Derby Fever." Symptomatic of the fever is the victim's uncontrollable urge to attend every event, public and private, to which he can wangle an invitation. That includes The Great Steamboat Race, the Pegasus Parade, and the Great Balloon Race for starters, and uncounted parties at clubs and homes throughout the surrounding Louisville area.

Then, on the Big Day, with his remaining strength, the horse fancier dresses rakishly and goes out to Churchill Downs. Relying heavily on conflicting advice, he puts down his money and positions himself to watch the year's top three-year-old thoroughbreds flash around the mile-and-a-quarter oval in the Run For The Roses, most famous horse race in the world.

Whether his horse wins or not, he'll see the blanket made of 500 red roses draped over the winner's neck, hear the Governor make a little speech, and see the winner's owner hug the jockey.

Racing program cover, 1883.

Baked Kentucky Ham with Beaten Biscuits, Marinated Vegetable Salad, Turkey Hash with Cornbread Waffles, Green Beans Southern Style, and Bloody Marys.

DERBY BRUNCH

Every Kentucky Derby hostess possesses a GRAM (Generally Recognized as Mandatory) list of foods to be served at Derby parties. The list consists of country ham, biscuits, grits, Kentucky Limestone bibb lettuce, fresh asparagus, and fresh strawberries. By the time the day ends, the well-fed guests will almost certainly have tasted all of them at least once.

Our brunch menu pre-supposes that you will have strawberries in another context that day, perhaps in your breakfast champagne or from a silver bowl with bourbon and powdered sugar for dipping them.

BLOODY MARYS
BAKED KENTUCKY HAM * COMMERCIAL BEATEN
BISCUITS
TURKEY HASH WITH CORNMEAL WAFFLES
PICKLED JERUSALEM ARTICHOKES
MARINATED VEGETABLE SALAD
GREEN BEANS SOUTHERN STYLE
JOCKEY'S REWARD PIE

Serves 24

Churchill Downs Museum

BLOODY MARYS

2 (46-ounce) cans tomato juice
3 cups vodka
Juice of 8 lemons
2 tablespoons Worcestershire sauce
1 teaspoon salt
1 teaspoon pepper
½ to 1 teaspoon hot sauce
¼ cup lemon or lime juice
¼ cup plus 2 tablespoons coarse salt
Ice cubes
Thin lime slices

Combine tomato juice, vodka, lemon juice, Worcestershire sauce, salt, pepper, and hot sauce; stir well. Chill thoroughly.

Place ¼ cup lemon or lime juice in a saucer. Place coarse salt in another saucer. Spin rim of each glass in juice and then in salt. Carefully place ice cubes in glass; pour Bloody Mary mixture over ice. Garnish each serving with a lime slice. Yield: 24 servings.

*Dressed up for The Derby.
Program cover, 1885.*

BAKED KENTUCKY HAM

1 (14- to 15-pound) country ham
1 cup red wine vinegar
1 cup firmly packed brown sugar
2 cups firmly packed dark brown sugar
2 tablespoons yellow cornmeal
2 tablespoons dry mustard
Commercial beaten biscuits

Scrub ham thoroughly with a stiff brush. Place ham in a very large container; cover with water. Add vinegar and 1 cup brown sugar. Cover and bring to a boil. Reduce heat, and cook 3 hours and 20 minutes.

Allow ham to cool in cooking liquid. Remove ham from liquid; remove skin. Place ham, fat side up, on a cutting board; score fat in a diamond design.

Place ham in a shallow roasting pan. Combine dark brown sugar, cornmeal, and mustard; pat over surface of ham, coating well. Bake at 350° for 20 minutes or until glaze is melted. Cover and chill in refrigerator overnight. Cut into paper thin slices. Serve with beaten biscuits. Yield: about 30 servings.

Note: Leftover ham may be refrigerated for later use.

From Frank Leslie's Illustrated Newspaper, *May 4, 1872.*

TURKEY HASH WITH CORNMEAL WAFFLES

1 (12- to 14-pound) turkey
2 tablespoons salt, divided
1½ teaspoons pepper, divided
1 pound hot bulk pork sausage
8 stalks celery, chopped
2 medium onions, chopped
¼ cup butter or margarine
6 cups cornbread crumbs
10 slices bread, dried and crumbled
½ pound fresh mushrooms, sliced
1 tablespoon rubbed sage
About 5 cups broth
Cornmeal Waffles

Remove giblets and neck from turkey; reserve liver for other uses. Simmer neck and gizzard in 2 quarts salted water to make broth. Rinse turkey thoroughly with cold water; pat dry. Combine 1 tablespoon salt and 1 teaspoon pepper; sprinkle over surface and in cavity of turkey.

Cook sausage until browned; drain well. Sauté celery and onion in butter until tender. Combine sausage, sautéed vegetables, cornbread crumbs, breadcrumbs, mushrooms, sage, and remaining salt and pepper in a large mixing bowl; mix well. Add broth, and stir until all ingredients are moistened. Stuff dressing into cavity of turkey.

Place turkey, breast side up, in a large, deep roasting pan. Lift wingtips up and over back, tucking securely under bird. Spoon remaining dressing around and over bird. Cover tightly with lid. Bake at 325° for about 4 hours or until turkey is "fall-apart" tender. Turkey is done when drumsticks can be pulled away from turkey.

Remove turkey from roaster; let stand until cool to the touch. Remove dressing from cavity of turkey. Bone and coarsely chop turkey. Combine chopped meat and dressing in a large mixing bowl, stirring well. Add more broth, if necessary. Serve over Cornmeal Waffles. Yield: 24 servings.

Cornmeal Waffles:

5 cups self-rising cornmeal
1 cup self-rising flour
5 cups boiling water
1¾ cups milk
4 eggs
⅓ cup bacon drippings

Combine cornmeal and flour; add boiling water, and let stand 10 minutes. Add milk, eggs, and bacon drippings, mixing well.

Pour about 1⅓ cups batter onto a hot, lightly oiled 9-inch waffle iron. Cook 5 minutes or until golden brown. Repeat procedure until all batter is used. Break waffles into fourths; cut each in half. Yield: about 4 dozen.

PICKLED JERUSALEM ARTICHOKES

1½ pounds Jerusalem
   artichokes
4 cups water
¼ cup coarse salt
2 small onions, thinly sliced
2 cups vinegar
1½ cups sugar
10 whole cloves
1 (2-inch) stick cinnamon
1 clove garlic
1 tablespoon mustard seeds
1 teaspoon celery seeds
½ teaspoon crushed red
   pepper

Scrub artichokes thoroughly
with a stiff brush; cut into thin
slices. Combine water and salt,
stirring to dissolve. Add artichokes and onion; cover and refrigerate overnight. Drain
artichokes and onion; set aside.

Combine remaining ingre-
dients in a saucepan; bring to a
boil and cook 5 minutes, stirring occasionally. Remove cinnamon, garlic, and cloves.

Spoon artichokes and onion
into hot sterilized jars; pour hot
vinegar mixture over vegetables,
leaving ¼-inch headspace.
Cover at once with metal lids,
and screw bands tight. Process
in boiling-water bath 5 minutes. Yield: 2 pints.

Note: Pickled artichokes
should be stored in a cool place
at least 2 weeks before using.

THREE POUNDS

JOCKEY CLUB

BRAND

PURE

MARINATED VEGETABLE SALAD

1 (1½-pound) bunch fresh
   broccoli
1 (10-ounce) package frozen
   asparagus spears, cut into
   2-inch diagonal slices
1 large head cauliflower,
   broken into flowerets
3 small zucchini, sliced
2 medium cucumbers, sliced
Marinade (recipe follows)
3 heads Bibb lettuce,
   separated into leaves
Tomato wedges

Trim broccoli; wash and
break off flowerets. Reserve
stalks for other uses.

Arrange broccoli in steaming
rack; place over boiling water.
Cover and steam 5 minutes. Remove from rack; set aside to
cool. Repeat procedure with asparagus and cauliflower.

Place steamed vegetables
under cold running water;
drain. Combine with zucchini
and cucumber in a large plastic
bag. Pour marinade over vegetables. Fasten bag securely.
Gently turn bag until vegetable
pieces are coated. Refrigerate
several hours or overnight,
turning bag once or twice.

To serve, cut corner from bag,
place over colander, and let
drain thoroughly. Line salad
bowl with Bibb lettuce; empty
bag of drained vegetables into
bowl. Garnish with tomato
wedges. Yield: 24 servings.

Marinade:

1¼ cups vegetable oil
¼ cup plus 2 tablespoons
   lemon juice
3 tablespoons vinegar
¾ teaspoon Worcestershire
   sauce
⅛ teaspoon hot sauce
2 small cloves garlic, minced
1½ teaspoons grated onion
¾ teaspoon pepper

Combine all ingredients; mix
well. Yield: about 2 cups.

*"Jockey Club," a coffee
product of New Orleans.*

GREEN BEANS SOUTHERN STYLE

6 pounds fresh green beans
1 (1-pound) pork jowl bacon
8 cups water
2 medium-size red pepper
   pods
1 tablespoon plus 1 teaspoon
   salt
½ teaspoon pepper

Remove strings from beans.
Cut beans into 2-inch pieces;
wash and set aside.

Remove rind from bacon and
discard rind. Cut off three ½-
inch slices from bacon, and set
aside. Cut remaining bacon into
½-inch cubes; set aside.

Place beans, reserved bacon
slices, water, and red pepper
pods in a Dutch oven. Cover and
bring to a boil. Reduce heat;
simmer 2½ hours. Add salt and
pepper; cook 30 minutes or
until tender.

Place cubed bacon in a small
skillet; cook over medium heat
until crisp. Drain well. Garnish
beans with fried bacon cubes.
Yield: about 24 servings.

JOCKEY'S REWARD PIE

9 eggs, beaten
3 cups firmly packed brown
   sugar
1½ cups light corn syrup
¼ cup plus 2 tablespoons
   all-purpose flour
1½ teaspoons vanilla extract
3 cups chopped walnuts
3 cups semisweet chocolate
   morsels
3 unbaked 9-inch pastry
   shells
3 cups whipping cream,
   whipped

Combine first 4 ingredients;
beat well. Stir in vanilla. Sprinkle walnuts and chocolate morsels into pastry shells; pour egg
mixture over walnuts and chocolate morsels. Bake at 425° for
10 minutes. Reduce temperature to 350°; bake 30 minutes.
Cool. Garnish with dollops of
whipped cream. Yield: three 9-
inch pies.

AFTER THE RACE

After the Race, parties are an indispensable part of the Derby Festival; they give winners a chance to chortle over their luck, while losers take the occasion to nurse their depression in a supportive atmosphere. The losers are quieter, but have this in common with the winners: they're uniformly hungry and thirsty.

Speaking of thirst, Kentucky's mint julep heritage goes back to the days when Kentucky was a county of Virginia. Virginians were accustomed not only to eating well, but also to drinking well. Many of them, including some of our presidents, had their own distilleries. President Tyler was particularly fond of mint juleps. When many juleps are to be served, it saves time to use simple syrup instead of sugar in muddling the mint.

SHRIMP PUFFS
CAVIAR CANAPÉS
MINI PIZZAS
PARTY QUICHES
DEVILED SWEETBREADS
STUFFED CLAMS
ESCARGOTS
RUMAKI
KENTUCKY MINT JULEP

Serves 20

SHRIMP PUFFS

1 cup water
½ cup butter
1 cup all-purpose flour
4 eggs
2 (6-ounce) packages frozen cooked shrimp, thawed and drained
½ cup mayonnaise
¼ cup finely chopped celery hearts
¼ cup finely chopped green pepper
¼ cup finely chopped red pepper
2 tablespoons chopped green onion
2 tablespoons sweet pickle relish
½ teaspoon salt
¼ teaspoon pepper

Combine water and butter in a saucepan; bring to a boil. Add flour, stirring vigorously over low heat 1 minute or until mixture leaves sides of pan and forms a smooth ball. Remove from heat; let cool slightly.

Add eggs, one at a time, beating with a wooden spoon after each addition; beat until batter is smooth. Drop by teaspoonfuls about 2 inches apart on ungreased baking sheets.

Bake at 425° for 20 minutes or until golden brown and puffed. Cool away from drafts on wire racks. Cut top off mini puffs; pull out and discard soft dough inside. Reserve tops.

Set aside ¼ cup shrimp; finely chop remaining shrimp. Add chopped shrimp to remaining ingredients, mixing well. Spoon 1 heaping teaspoon of shrimp mixture into mini puffs; replace tops. Arrange on serving platter, and garnish with reserved shrimp. Yield: about 4 dozen.

Note: Other chopped seafood, ham, or chicken may be substituted for shrimp.

CAVIAR CANAPÉS

12 slices bread
1 (8-ounce) package cream cheese, softened
1 cup finely chopped fresh parsley
1 (2-ounce) jar red caviar
1 (2-ounce) jar black caviar

Lightly toast each side of bread; trim crust. Using a small diamond-shaped cookie cutter, cut 2 shapes from each slice. Spread each slice with softened cream cheese, and dip edges in chopped parsley.

Place about ½ teaspoon red caviar in the center of 12 of the canapés. Repeat procedure with black caviar and remaining canapés. Transfer to serving platter. Yield: 2 dozen.

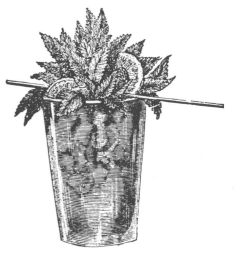

MINI PIZZAS

1 (1-pound) loaf unsliced
French bread
1 (14-ounce) jar commercial
pizza sauce
¾ cup finely chopped ripe
olives
¾ cup finely chopped
pepperoni
¾ cup finely chopped fresh
mushrooms
1½ cups (6 ounces) shredded
mozzarella cheese

Cut bread into ¼-inch-thick slices; cut slices into rounds with a 2-inch cookie cutter. Spread each round with pizza sauce. Top evenly with olives, pepperoni, and mushrooms; sprinkle with cheese.

Place pizzas on ungreased baking sheets. Bake at 350° for 3 to 5 minutes. Serve warm. Yield: about 3 dozen.

PARTY QUICHES

½ cup chopped onion
1½ teaspoons butter or
margarine
½ pound sliced bacon
½ cup (2 ounces) shredded
Swiss cheese
4 eggs, beaten
1 cup pancake mix
½ cup half-and-half
¼ teaspoon salt
⅛ teaspoon pepper

Sauté onion in butter in a small skillet until tender, and set aside.

Cook bacon in a large skillet until crisp; drain bacon on paper towels. Crumble and set aside; discard drippings.

Combine onion, bacon, and cheese; sprinkle mixture evenly among 3 greased miniature muffin pans.

Combine eggs, pancake mix, half-and-half, salt, and pepper; stir well. Pour mixture evenly into prepared muffin pans, filling two-thirds full. Bake at 400° for 15 minutes or until tops of quiches are lightly browned. Remove from muffin pans; cool 5 minutes on wire racks. Yield: 3 dozen.

DEVILED SWEETBREADS

1 pound veal sweetbreads
1 cup chopped celery
½ cup chopped onion
1 tablespoon lemon juice
1 large bay leaf, broken
12 peppercorns
1 teaspoon salt
5 cups water
½ pound fresh mushrooms,
sliced
¼ cup butter or margarine,
melted
¼ cup all-purpose flour
¼ cup sherry
2 cups milk
1 tablespoon Dijon mustard
2 teaspoons thick steak sauce
Toast points

Soak sweetbreads in ice water to cover for 30 minutes. Drain well, and set aside.

Combine celery, onion, lemon juice, bay leaf, peppercorns, and salt in a Dutch oven. Stir in water; bring to a boil. Reduce heat; simmer 5 minutes.

Add sweetbreads to broth; reduce heat, and simmer 30 minutes. Drain sweetbreads, discarding broth and other ingredients.

Immediately cover sweetbreads with ice water, and cool completely. Drain off water; remove and discard white membrane and tubes. Cube sweetbreads and set aside.

Sauté mushrooms in butter in a large skillet; stir in flour. Cook 1 minute, stirring constantly. Gradually add sherry and milk; cook over medium heat, stirring constantly, until thickened and bubbly. Reduce heat. Add mustard and steak sauce, blending well. Stir in sweetbreads.

Serve over toast points. Yield: 20 appetizer servings.

STUFFED CLAMS

⅔ cup finely chopped
celery
⅔ cup finely chopped fresh
mushrooms
⅓ cup finely chopped green
pepper
2 tablespoons chopped green
onion
1 tablespoon chopped fresh
parsley
2 tablespoons butter or
margarine
1½ tablespoons all-purpose
flour
1 (6½-ounce) can minced
clams, undrained
1 egg, beaten
1 teaspoon lemon juice
¼ teaspoon salt
⅛ teaspoon garlic powder
20 clam shells
1 cup soft breadcrumbs
¼ cup grated Parmesan
cheese
¼ cup butter or margarine,
melted
¼ cup chopped fresh
parsley
1 teaspoon paprika
Rock salt

Sauté celery, mushrooms, green pepper, green onion, and 1 tablespoon parsley in 2 tablespoons butter. Stir in flour, and cook 1 additional minute. Add clams and cook until thickened, stirring constantly.

Gradually stir about one-fourth of clam mixture into egg; add egg mixture to remaining clam mixture, stirring constantly. Stir in lemon juice, salt, and garlic powder. Place 1 tablespoon of clam mixture into greased clam shells. Set clam shells aside.

Combine breadcrumbs, cheese, and melted butter; toss lightly. Sprinkle crumb mixture evenly over clam mixture. Top with ¼ cup parsley, and sprinkle with paprika.

To bake, pour enough rock salt into a 13- x 9- x 2-inch baking dish to cover bottom (salt helps shells sit upright); arrange filled shells on salt. Bake at 400° for 10 minutes or until lightly browned. Yield: 20 appetizer servings.

RUMAKI

12 chicken livers
12 water chestnuts
12 slices bacon
½ cup soy sauce
½ cup sherry
2 tablespoons finely
   chopped onion
1 tablespoon brown
   sugar
2 cloves garlic, minced
2 teaspoons grated fresh
   gingerroot
¼ teaspoon hot sauce

Cut chicken livers, water chestnuts, and bacon in half. Place a chicken liver half and a water chestnut half on each half of bacon. Roll up and secure with a wooden pick, making sure pick goes through water chestnut. Place in a shallow baking dish.

Combine remaining ingredients; stir until sugar dissolves. Pour marinade over prepared rumaki; let stand at room temperature 1 hour, turning twice. Drain well on paper towels.

Place rumaki on a rack in a broiler pan. Broil until bacon is crisp, turning frequently to brown all sides. Yield: 2 dozen.

From bottom left clockwise: Quiches, Shrimp Puffs, Mint Juleps, Smoked Salmon, Rumaki, Mini Pizzas, Deviled Sweetbreads, Escargots, Stuffed Clams, and Caviar Canapés.

ESCARGOTS

2 cups butter or margarine,
   softened
¼ cup coarsely chopped fresh
   parsley
2 tablespoons chopped green
   onion
1½ tablespoons minced garlic
1 teaspoon salt
½ teaspoon pepper
1 tablespoon Pernod
   (optional)
½ cup soft breadcrumbs
¼ cup Chablis or other dry
   white wine
2 (7½-ounce) cans snails,
   drained and rinsed
24 snail shells, rinsed and
   drained
Additional soft breadcrumbs
Rock salt (optional)
Fresh parsley sprigs

Combine softened butter, parsley, green onion, garlic, salt, pepper, and Pernod, if desired, in a large mixing bowl; blend well.

Combine ½ cup breadcrumbs and wine; add to butter mixture, mixing well.

Fill shells half full with seasoned butter. Place snails in shells. Pack remainder of each shell with seasoned butter. Sprinkle with breadcrumbs.

Place shells in snail pans, or pour rock salt into a 13- x 9- x 2-inch baking dish to cover bottom (salt helps shells sit upright); arrange shells, open end up, on salt. Bake at 375° for 10 to 12 minutes. Garnish with parsley sprigs. Yield: 2 dozen.

KENTUCKY MINT JULEP

1 teaspoon sugar
1 teaspoon water
4 fresh mint leaves
Finely crushed ice
3 ounces bourbon
1 fresh mint sprig

Combine first 3 ingredients in a chilled julep cup; mull gently until sugar dissolves.

Add enough finely crushed ice to fill cup three-fourths full. Add bourbon, and stir gently. Add additional crushed ice to fill cup. Freeze for at least 15 minutes. Before serving, garnish with a fresh mint sprig. Yield: 1 serving.

Note: Mint Juleps should be made individually and preferably in a julep cup.

Fourth of July

Those were dangerous times, that summer of 1776, as the Continental Congress debated whether or not to declare independence. The British generals were closing in, Howe nearing New York and Burboyne already victorious in Canada. Richard Henry Lee decided the time had come, and he introduced a resolution "...that these United Colonies are, and of right ought to be, free and independent states. . . ."

Five men, Thomas Jefferson, John Adams, Benjamin Franklin, Philip Livingston, and Roger Sherman were asked to "embody the spirit and purpose," and Jefferson set about writing the document.

Late on July 4, 1776, the vote was taken. Nine colonies voted in favor: John Hancock signed it to make it official, and broadsides were published. The first anniversary of the signing was celebrated in Philadelphia in 1777 with ringing bells, booming cannons, and fireworks. The struggle for independence was not over, but the spirit had been established. Let's celebrate!

A smiling Uncle Sam sets an example for fireworks to celebrate Independence Day in this colorful greeting card dating back to 1907.

STARS AND STRIPES PICNIC

On the "Glorious Fourth," sometime between the fried chicken and the ice cream, perhaps we should give a solemn thought to the flag that waves over the proceedings. In the 1840s, down in Pike County, Mississippi, a historian recorded:

"...Old Glory waved proudly from a staff a hundred feet high. The music of fife and drum and the parading of volunteer companies. . .stirred their patriotic ardor. . . ."

We can recapture the spirit with our traditional picnic and dressed up blueberry cake.

GOLDEN FRIED CHICKEN
CORN ON THE COB
DILL PICKLES
RADISHES
PICNIC ROLLS
PICKLED PEACHES
WATERMELON FRUIT BASKET
STARS AND STRIPES BLUEBERRY CAKE
SOUR CREAM CHOCOLATE CHIP COOKIES
PEPPERMINT STICK ICE CREAM
APPLE LEMONADE

Serves 12

Picnic on the Fourth of July, *engraving by Samuel Hollyer after Lilly M. Spencer, 1864.*

Library of Congress

GOLDEN FRIED CHICKEN

3 cups all-purpose flour
1½ teaspoons salt
¾ teaspoon pepper
¾ teaspoon paprika
1½ teaspoons baking soda
3 cups buttermilk
3 (2½- to 3-pound) broiler
 fryers, cut up
Vegetable oil

Combine flour, salt, pepper, and paprika in a plastic or paper bag; shake to mix, and set aside. Dissolve soda in the buttermilk; set aside.

Place 2 or 3 pieces of chicken in bag; shake well. Dip chicken into buttermilk mixture. Return chicken to flour mixture, coating well. Repeat procedure with remaining chicken.

Heat 1 inch of oil in a large skillet to 350°; add several pieces of chicken, and fry 25 minutes or until golden brown, turning once. Repeat procedure. Drain chicken well on paper towels. Yield: 12 servings.

CORN ON THE COB

12 ears fresh corn
6 to 6½ quarts water
2 tablespoons salt
Butter or margarine
Salt and pepper to taste

Remove husks and silks from corn just before cooking. Combine water and salt in a large Dutch oven; stir to dissolve salt. Bring water to a boil, and add corn. Return water to a boil; cover and cook 15 to 20 minutes. Drain well. Serve with butter and salt and pepper to taste. Yield: 12 servings.

PICNIC ROLLS

2 packages dry yeast
1 cup warm water (105°
 to 115°)
1 cup milk
¼ cup plus 1 tablespoon
 sugar
1 tablespoon salt
About 7 cups all-purpose
 flour, divided
¼ cup plus 2 tablespoons
 shortening, melted
1 egg, beaten
Melted butter or margarine

Dissolve yeast in warm water. Let stand 5 minutes or until bubbly; set aside.

Scald milk in a small saucepan; add sugar and salt, and let cool to lukewarm. Combine dissolved yeast and milk mixture in a large mixing bowl; mix well.

Add 3 cups flour; beat until smooth. Add shortening and egg; beat well. Add enough remaining flour to make a soft dough.

Turn dough out onto a lightly floured surface, and knead 8 minutes or until smooth and elastic. Place dough in a well-greased bowl, turning to grease top. Cover and let rise in a warm place (85°), free from drafts, 1½ hours or until doubled in bulk.

Punch dough down. Shape into 1½-inch balls; place in two lightly greased 9-inch square pans. Cover and repeat rising procedure 45 minutes or until doubled in bulk. Bake at 400° for 12 minutes or until golden brown. Brush tops with melted butter. Yield: about 2 dozen.

PICKLED PEACHES

3 cups sugar
2 cups vinegar
½ teaspoon ground cinnamon
½ teaspoon ground cloves
3½ pounds firm, ripe peaches,
 peeled

Combine sugar, vinegar, and spices in a large Dutch oven; bring to a boil. Add peaches; cover and simmer 8 minutes or until slightly tender.

Remove peaches from syrup using a slotted spoon, and pack into hot sterilized jars, leaving ½-inch headspace. Cover peaches with boiling syrup, leaving ½-inch headspace. Adjust lids; process pints for 20 minutes and quarts for 25 minutes in boiling-water bath. Yield: 4 pints or 2 quarts.

Watermelon feast in Kittrell, North Carolina, c.1900.

WATERMELON FRUIT BASKET

1 (18-pound) watermelon
2 cups honeydew balls
2 cups cantaloupe balls
2 cups strawberries
Fresh mint leaves

Cut watermelon in half crosswise. Cut a thin slice from the bottom of one watermelon half so that it will sit flat, being careful not to cut through melon. (Reserve remaining half of watermelon for other uses.)

Draw 1-inch notches around cut edge of top of watermelon. Cut out notches using a sharp knife, and discard.

Scoop watermelon into balls to yield about 8 cups, leaving a ½-inch margin of fruit around rind to form shell; remove seeds.

Combine watermelon balls, remaining fruit balls, and strawberries; toss lightly to distribute evenly. Spoon fruit into watermelon shell. Garnish with mint leaves. Yield: 12 servings.

STARS AND STRIPES BLUEBERRY CAKE

3 cups sifted cake flour
2 teaspoons baking powder
1¾ cups sugar
1½ teaspoons salt
1 cup shortening
¾ cup milk
4 eggs
2 teaspoons vanilla extract
2 cups fresh blueberries, rinsed and drained
Cream Cheese Frosting
Maraschino cherries, quartered
Fresh blueberries

Sift together flour, baking powder, sugar, and salt. Add shortening, milk, and 2 eggs; beat 2 minutes at medium speed of electric mixer. Add remaining 2 eggs, beating well. Stir in vanilla, and fold in 2 cups blueberries.

Pour batter into a greased and floured 13- x 9- x 2-inch baking pan. Bake at 350° for 45 minutes or until a wooden pick inserted in center comes out clean. Cool in pan 10 to 15 minutes; remove from pan, and let cool completely.

Spread Cream Cheese Frosting on top and sides of cake. Decorate cake with rows of cherries and blueberries. Yield: one 13- x 9-inch cake.

Cream Cheese Frosting:

1 (8-ounce) package cream cheese, softened
2 tablespoons milk
1 (16-ounce) package powdered sugar, sifted

Beat cream cheese until light and fluffy; gradually add remaining ingredients, beating well. Yield: enough for one 13- x 9-inch cake.

Uncle Sam and Miss Liberty pose with costumed friends.

SOUR CREAM CHOCOLATE CHIP COOKIES

1 cup butter or margarine, softened
¾ cup firmly packed brown sugar
¾ cup sugar
2 eggs
½ cup commercial sour cream
1 teaspoon vanilla extract
2¼ cups all-purpose flour
1 teaspoon baking soda
½ teaspoon salt
1 (6-ounce) package semisweet chocolate morsels
1½ cups coarsely chopped pecans

Cream butter; gradually add sugar, beating well. Add eggs, sour cream, and vanilla, beating well. Combine flour, soda, and salt; add to creamed mixture, blending well. Stir in chocolate morsels and pecans.

Drop dough by tablespoonfuls onto lightly greased baking sheets. Bake at 375° for 10 to 12 minutes. Cool slightly on baking sheets; remove to wire racks, and let cool completely. Yield: about 2½ dozen.

PEPPERMINT STICK ICE CREAM

3 eggs
¾ cup sugar
3 cups whipping cream
2 cups milk
1 cup half-and-half
2 cups crushed peppermint stick candy, divided
2 tablespoons vanilla extract
¼ teaspoon salt

Beat eggs until foamy; gradually add sugar, beating until thickened. Add whipping cream, milk, half-and-half, 1 cup candy, vanilla, and salt; stir well. Cover; refrigerate at least 12 hours to dissolve candy.

Pour mixture into freezer of a 1-gallon hand-turned or electric freezer. Freeze according to manufacturer's instructions. Stir in remaining 1 cup candy. Let ripen at least 1 hour. Yield: about 3 quarts.

APPLE LEMONADE

2½ quarts apple juice
1¾ cups plus 2 tablespoons fresh lemon juice
½ cup plus 2 tablespoons sugar
Ice Cubes
Lemon slices (optional)
Fresh mint leaves (optional)

Combine juices and sugar; stir until sugar dissolves. Chill thoroughly, and serve over ice. Garnish with lemon slices or mint leaves, if desired. Yield: about 12 cups.

BARBECUE, KENTUCKY STYLE

Of a Fourth of July picnic-barbecue on the banks of Beargrass Creek near Louisville in the early 1800s, John James Audubon wrote, "The whole neighborhood joined with one consent. Each denizen had freely given his ox, his ham, his venison, his turkeys, and other fowls. . .flagons of every beverage used in the country. The melons of all sorts, peaches, plums, and pears, would have sufficed to stock a market. In a word, Kentucky, the land of abundance, had supplied a feast for her children.

"A great wooden cannon was now crammed with home-made powder, fire was conveyed to it, and as the explosion burst forth, thousands of hearty huzzas mingled with its echoes. My spirit is refreshed every 4th of July by the recollection of that day's merriment. . . ."

KENTUCKY BURGOO
WESTERN KENTUCKY-STYLE BARBECUE SAUCE
BARBECUED PORK RIBS
BARBECUED CHICKEN
MOLDED POTATO SALAD
DRESSED CUCUMBERS
BRITTLE BROWN SUGAR COOKIES

Serves 12

KENTUCKY BURGOO

- 1 pound pork shank
- 1 pound veal shank
- 1 pound beef shank
- 1 pound breast of lamb
- 1 (5- to 5½-pound) baking hen
- 4 quarts water
- 3 cups peeled, cubed potatoes
- 2 cups chopped onion
- 1 cup chopped carrots
- 1 cup diced celery
- 2 medium-size green peppers, chopped
- 2 (28-ounce) cans whole tomatoes, drained and chopped
- 2 cups fresh or frozen corn
- 2 cups fresh or frozen butterbeans
- 1 dried red pepper pod, crushed
- 1 tablespoon plus 1 teaspoon Worcestershire sauce
- 1½ teaspoons salt
- ¼ cup chopped fresh parsley

Combine first six ingredients in a large stock pot. Bring to a boil. Reduce heat; cover and simmer 3 hours. Remove all meat from broth. Cool. Remove meat from bones, and cut into pieces. Return meat to broth.

American Museum of Natural History

Add remaining ingredients; stir well. Simmer, uncovered, 5 hours, stirring occasionally. Yield: 12 servings.

Artist John James Audubon wrote about life in the Mississippi and Ohio Valleys in the early 1800s.

WESTERN KENTUCKY-STYLE BARBECUE SAUCE

1¾ cups water
1 cup plus 2 tablespoons catsup
¼ cup plus 2 tablespoons Worcestershire sauce
1 teaspoon paprika
1 teaspoon dry mustard
¾ teaspoon garlic salt
¾ teaspoon onion powder
1½ teaspoons red pepper
¾ teaspoon pepper

Combine all ingredients in a large saucepan, mixing well. Bring to a boil; reduce heat to medium. Cook, uncovered, 20 minutes, stirring occasionally. Use sauce to baste chicken or ribs. Yield: about 1 quart.

BARBECUED PORK RIBS

6 pounds spareribs
Western Kentucky-Style Barbecue Sauce

Cut spareribs into serving-size pieces (about 3 to 4 ribs per person).
Place ribs, bone side down, on grill over slow coals. Grill 1½ hours, turning frequently. Brush ribs with Western Kentucky-Style Barbecue Sauce, and cook 10 to 15 additional minutes on each side. Yield: 12 servings.

BARBECUED CHICKEN

3 (3- to 3½-pound) broiler-fryers, split
Western Kentucky-Style Barbecue Sauce

Place chicken, skin side down, on grill. Grill over medium coals 50 minutes or until tender, turning chicken every 10 minutes.
Brush with Western Kentucky-Style Barbecue Sauce during last 20 minutes. Yield: 6 servings.

MOLDED POTATO SALAD

12 medium-size new potatoes
1½ cups diced celery
3 tablespoons chopped onion
2½ tablespoons chopped sweet pickle
3 tablespoons sweet pickle juice
3 hard-cooked eggs, chopped
1½ cups mayonnaise
¾ teaspoon salt
½ teaspoon pepper
Lettuce leaves
1 hard-cooked egg, sliced
Pimiento strips

Cook potatoes in boiling water about 30 minutes or until potatoes are tender. Drain well and cool. Peel potatoes, and cut into ½-inch cubes.
Combine potatoes, celery, onion, pickle, pickle juice, chopped egg, salt, pepper, and mayonnaise in a large mixing bowl; toss lightly to coat well.
Line a 2½-quart mixing bowl with plastic wrap. Spoon potato mixture into bowl, pressing gently to mold. Cover and refrigerate at least 1 hour. Unmold potato salad onto a lettuce-lined platter. Garnish with egg slices and pimiento strips. Yield: 12 servings.

DRESSED CUCUMBERS

4 large cucumbers, unpeeled and thinly sliced
2 small onions, separated into rings
2 medium-size green peppers, chopped
¼ cup chopped fresh parsley
1 cup apple cider vinegar
1 cup water
¼ cup sugar
1 tablespoon salt
½ teaspoon pepper
Lettuce leaves

Combine first 4 ingredients in a shallow dish; toss lightly.
Combine next 5 ingredients, mixing well. Pour over vegetables, tossing to coat well. Cover and chill at least 2 hours. Drain and serve in a lettuce-lined bowl. Yield: 12 servings.

BRITTLE BROWN SUGAR COOKIES

1 cup butter, softened
2 cups sugar
1 cup firmly packed brown sugar
3 eggs
1 teaspoon baking soda
1 tablespoon water
5 cups all-purpose flour
1 teaspoon baking powder
2 tablespoons ground cinnamon
1½ tablespoons lemon juice
1 cup finely chopped pecans

Cream butter; gradually add sugar, beating well. Add eggs, one at a time, beating well after each addition.
Dissolve soda in water. Add to creamed mixture, mixing well. Combine next 3 ingredients; gradually add to creamed mixture, mixing well. Stir in lemon juice and pecans. Shape dough into a ball. Cover and refrigerate 45 minutes.
Turn dough out onto a floured surface, and roll to ⅛-inch thickness; cut dough with cookie cutters. Place on lightly greased baking sheets. Bake at 400° for 8 minutes. Cool on wire racks. Yield: about 5 dozen.

OLD-FASHIONED ICE CREAM SOCIAL

While ice cream was not common in the late eighteenth-century American home, it was not unknown. George Washington, who may have learned about it from the Marquis de Lafayette, had an ice cream freezer as early as 1784. But it was Thomas Jefferson who became enamored of ice cream while in France and brought back recipes for delicate ices as well as for rich frozen creams. In 1791, he is said to have ordered 50 vanilla pods from Paris, some of which were presumably used in the making of vanilla-flavored ice cream.

Certainly these founding fathers would think an ice cream social an ideal way to celebrate the nation's birthday. Prepare freezers of everyone's favorite flavors, add cookies and cake, and presto! It's a party.

FRESH PEACH ICE CREAM
VANILLA ICE CREAM
CHOCOLATE ICE CREAM
ICE CREAM WAFERS
POUND CAKE

Serves 12

Happiness was the ice cream man on a hot July Fourth, Washington, D.C., 1920s.

Choose a flavor or have all three! Fresh Peach, Chocolate, and Vanilla Ice Cream with Pound Cake and Ice Cream Wafers.

VANILLA ICE CREAM

1 cup sugar
¼ cup plus 2 tablespoons all-purpose flour
¼ teaspoon salt
¼ cup plus 2 tablespoons milk
2 quarts milk, scalded
2 eggs, beaten
1 cup sugar
2 cups whipping cream
2 tablespoons vanilla extract

Combine first 4 ingredients in a Dutch oven. Gradually stir in scalded milk. Cook 20 minutes over medium heat, stirring constantly with a wire whisk.

Combine eggs and 1 cup sugar. Gradually stir a small amount of hot milk mixture into egg mixture. Add egg-milk mixture to remaining hot milk mixture; stir constantly. Remove from heat; cool completely. Chill at least 2 hours.

Add whipping cream and vanilla to chilled mixture, stirring with a wire whisk to combine.

Pour mixture into freezer can of a 1-gallon hand-turned or electric freezer. Freeze according to manufacturer's instructions. Let ripen 1½ to 2 hours. Yield: about 3 quarts.

CHOCOLATE ICE CREAM

Combine four (1-ounce) squares of semisweet chocolate and ¼ cup hot water in top of a double boiler; place over boiling water, stirring until chocolate melts. Proceed as directed for Vanilla Ice Cream (above); add melted chocolate mixture to scalded milk-sugar mixture after the latter has cooked 20 minutes. Yield: about 3 quarts.

FRESH PEACH ICE CREAM

6 eggs
1½ cups sugar
½ cup firmly packed brown sugar
1½ tablespoons all-purpose flour
Dash of salt
1 quart milk
¼ cup light corn syrup
5 cups sliced peaches, mashed
½ cup sugar
2 teaspoons vanilla extract
¼ teaspoon almond extract
1 (13-ounce) can evaporated milk, chilled

Beat eggs at medium speed of electric mixer until frothy. Gradually add 1½ cups sugar, brown sugar, flour, and salt; beat well. Stir in milk and syrup. Cook over low heat until mixture begins to thicken, stirring constantly. Remove from heat. Chill thoroughly.

Combine peaches and ½ cup sugar; stir well. Stir peaches into custard. Add flavorings.

Beat evaporated milk until soft peaks form; fold into custard mixture.

Pour mixture into freezer can of a 1-gallon hand-turned or electric freezer. Freeze according to manufactuer's instructions. Let ripen at least 1 hour before serving. Yield: 1 gallon.

ICE CREAM WAFERS

½ cup shortening
½ cup sugar
1 egg, beaten
¾ cup flour
½ teaspoon salt
½ teaspoon vanilla extract
½ cup pecan halves

Cream shortening; gradually add sugar, beating until light and fluffy. Add egg; beat well.

Combine flour and salt; add to creamed mixture, beating well. Stir in vanilla.

Drop batter by teaspoonfuls onto greased baking sheets. Press a pecan half in center of each cookie. Bake at 325° for 10 minutes or until lightly browned. Cool slightly on baking sheets; remove to wire racks, and let cool completely. Yield: about 2½ dozen.

POUND CAKE

1 cup butter, softened
3 cups sugar
6 eggs
3 cups all-purpose flour
1 cup whipping cream
2 teaspoons vanilla extract
1 teaspoon almond extract

Cream butter. Gradually add sugar; beat well. Add eggs, one at a time, beating well after each addition. Add flour to creamed mixture alternately with cream, beginning and ending with flour. Stir in flavorings.

Pour batter into a well-greased 10-inch tube pan. Bake at 350° for 1 hour and 25 minutes or until cake tests done. Cool in pan 20 minutes. Remove cake from pan, and place on wire rack, to cool completely. Yield: one 10-inch cake.

Above: Patriotic Lady of Mobile, c.1900.

Below: Fourth of July procession in Mobile, 1916.

Labor Day

Trade unions have an honorable history that goes back centuries to the European guilds. But it was not until 1882 that Peter J. McGuire, president of the United Brotherhood of Carpenters and Joiners of America, conceived the idea of setting aside one day a year in honor of the worker. He envisioned that on this day a parade would be held to show the strength and esprit de corps of the labor force. A picnic would then be held with proceeds going to the participants. He selected the date for Labor Day, the first Monday in September, because it fell midway between the Fourth of July and Thanksgiving.

The Central Labor Union adopted his proposal and suggested that the first Labor Day celebration take place September 5, 1882. It was voted to make the holiday a national one, and by June 28 of that year, Congress had passed it. Labor Day remains a day for parades, picnics, and generalized feasting.

Fannie Lou Spelce painted "County Memorial Fair" of 1908 from childhood memories.

Courtesy of Fannie Lou Spelce Associates

HOLIDAY COUNTY FAIR

If there is anything more American than apple pie, it is an apple pie baked for a county fair competition. Not to mention the other pies and cakes (jam cake is always a favorite), the canned fruits and vegetables, the cured hams. . . . Or do you most enjoy the well-groomed animals, or perhaps the handwork exhibits?

Neshoba County, Mississippi, has one of the longest running fairs in the South. It began as a community picnic in 1889. Since it was harvest time, people began to bring produce and livestock to show, and set up camp for several days. Meals such as this were cooked outdoors in iron utensils around the turn of the century.

NESHOBA COUNTY FRIED CHICKEN
BAKED COUNTRY-CURED HAM
PARSLEY BUTTERED NEW POTATOES
SAUTÉED CORN
CONFETTI STRING BEANS
GREEN ONIONS
PICKLES
MISSISSIPPI CORNBREAD
GINGERSNAPS
BUTTERMILK CUSTARD PIE
JAM CAKE

Serves 10 to 12

NESHOBA COUNTY FRIED CHICKEN

3 cups all-purpose flour
1 tablespoon salt
¾ teaspoon pepper
3 (3- to 3½-pound) broiler-fryers, cut-up
3 cups milk
Vegetable oil

Combine flour, salt, and pepper; mix well. Dip chicken, a few pieces at a time, in milk; dredge in flour mixture.

Heat 1 inch of oil in a large skillet to 375°; add chicken, and fry 25 minutes or until golden brown. Drain on paper towels. Yield: 10 to 12 servings.

BAKED COUNTRY-CURED HAM

1 (12- to 15-pound) country ham
½ cup firmly packed brown sugar
2 tablespoons pineapple juice
1 tablespoon honey
½ teaspoon dry mustard

Place ham in a very large container; cover with cold water, and soak overnight. Remove ham from water and drain. Scrub ham thoroughly with a stiff brush, and rinse well with cold water.

Replace ham in container, and cover with fresh cold water. Bring to a boil; reduce heat and simmer 5 to 6 hours, allowing 25 minutes per pound. Turn ham occasionally during cooking time. Cool. Carefully remove ham from water; remove skin.

Place ham, fat side up, on a cutting board; score fat in a diamond design. Place ham, fat side up, in a shallow roasting pan. Combine remaining ingredients, mixing well. Coat exposed portion of ham with glaze. Bake, uncovered, at 325° for 30 minutes. Transfer to serving platter; slice ham thinly. Yield: 24 to 30 servings.

Note: Leftover ham may be refrigerated for later use.

PARSLEY BUTTERED NEW POTATOES

3 pounds new potatoes
½ cup butter or margarine, melted
½ cup chopped fresh parsley
Salt and pepper to taste

Pare a 1-inch strip around center of each potato. Cover and cook in boiling salted water 40 minutes or until tender. Drain potatoes, and set aside.

Combine butter, parsley, and salt and pepper to taste; stir well. Pour mixture over potatoes, coating thoroughly. Yield: 10 to 12 servings.

MISSISSIPPI CORNBREAD

2 cups cornmeal
1 teaspoon baking soda
1 teaspoon salt
2 eggs, beaten
2 cups buttermilk
¼ cup plus 2 tablespoons bacon drippings

Combine cornmeal, soda, and salt; stir in eggs and buttermilk.

Heat bacon drippings in a 10-inch cast-iron skillet in a 400° oven for 3 minutes or until very hot. Coat skillet well with drippings. Pour any excess melted drippings into batter, and mix well.

Pour batter into hot skillet, and bake at 450° for 20 minutes or until bread is golden brown. Yield: 10 to 12 servings.

GINGERSNAPS

3¼ cups all-purpose flour
½ teaspoon baking soda
1½ teaspoons salt
1 tablespoon ground ginger
1 cup molasses
½ cup butter or margarine
½ cup sugar

Combine flour, soda, salt, and ginger in a large mixing bowl; set aside.

Bring molasses to a boil in a medium saucepan. Remove from heat; add butter, stirring until butter melts. Add molasses mixture to flour mixture, stirring well. Cover and refrigerate 1 hour.

Turn dough out onto a lightly floured surface. Roll dough into 1-inch balls; roll balls in sugar. Place 2 inches apart on ungreased baking sheets. Bake at 375° for 10 minutes. (Tops will crack.) Yield: about 3½ dozen.

Note: Dough may be rolled to ⅛-inch thickness, and cut with a 2-inch cookie cutter. Sprinkle tops with sugar before baking.

Fried chicken, sautéed corn, string beans, and gingersnaps: A hearty way to celebrate the winning of a blue ribbon at the county fair.

SAUTÉED CORN

12 ears fresh corn
¼ cup plus 2 tablespoons bacon drippings
1 cup water
1 teaspoon salt

Cut corn from cob, scraping cob to remove pulp.

Heat bacon drippings in a heavy skillet over medium heat; add corn, water, and salt. Cover and simmer 30 minutes, stirring occasionally. Uncover and cook an additional 30 minutes or until thickened. Yield: 10 to 12 servings.

CONFETTI STRING BEANS

3 (16-ounce) cans cut green beans, undrained
2 medium onions, finely chopped
3 strips bacon, finely chopped
3 medium tomatoes, unpeeled, seeded, and coarsely chopped
2 medium-size green peppers, chopped
½ teaspoon salt

Drain green beans, reserving ½ cup liquid; set aside.

Sauté onion and bacon in a heavy skillet until onion is tender. Combine beans, reserved liquid, tomatoes, green pepper, salt, and sautéed onion mixture in a Dutch oven. Cover and cook over low heat 30 minutes. Yield: 10 to 12 servings.

BUTTERMILK CUSTARD PIE

8 eggs, separated
2 cups sugar
1 cup all-purpose flour
¼ cup plus 2 tablespoons
  butter, melted
1 teaspoon baking soda
4 cups buttermilk
¼ cup lemon juice
2 teaspoons vanilla extract
2 unbaked 9-inch pastry
  shells
¾ cup sugar
1 teaspoon vanilla extract

Beat egg yolks until thick and lemon colored. Combine 2 cups sugar and flour; gradually add to egg yolks, beating well. Add butter, mixing well. Dissolve soda in buttermilk; add to egg mixture. Stir in lemon juice and 2 teaspoons vanilla. Pour mixture evenly into pastry shells.

Bake at 425° for 10 minutes; reduce temperature to 350°, and bake 40 minutes or until knife inserted in center comes out clean. Remove from oven.

Beat egg whites (at room temperature) until foamy in a large mixing bowl. Gradually add ¾ cup sugar, beating until stiff peaks form. Beat in 1 teaspoon vanilla. Spread meringue over filling, sealing to edge of pastry. Bake at 350° for 8 minutes or until lightly browned. Cool. Yield: two 9-inch pies.

Pastry:

2 cups all-purpose flour
1 teaspoon salt
2 teaspoons sugar
⅔ cup shortening
¾ to 1 cup ice water

Combine first 3 ingredients; cut in shortening until mixture resembles coarse meal. Sprinkle water evenly over flour mixture; stir with a fork until dry ingredients are moistened. Shape dough into a ball, and wrap in waxed paper; chill.

Divide dough. Roll out on a floured surface; place in two 9-inch piepans. Trim pastry, leaving 1-inch overhang. Fold loose edges under, and flute rim. Yield: two 9-inch pastry shells.

JAM CAKE

1½ cups all-purpose flour
1 teaspoon baking soda
1 teaspoon ground cinnamon
1 teaspoon ground cloves
1 cup sugar
½ cup butter or margarine,
  softened
3 eggs, beaten
½ cup buttermilk
1 cup grape jam
Frosting (recipe follows)

Sift together flour, soda, cinnamon, cloves, and sugar; set aside.

Cream butter in a large mixing bowl; add eggs and buttermilk, beating well. Add flour mixture and jam; beat at medium speed of electric mixer for 3 minutes.

Pour batter into 2 greased and floured 8-inch round cakepans. Bake at 350° for 30 minutes or until a wooden pick inserted in center comes out clean. Cool in pans 10 minutes; remove layers from pans, and cool completely on wire racks.

Spread frosting between layers and on top and sides of cake. Yield: one 2-layer cake.

Frosting:

3 cups sugar, divided
1 cup whipping cream
½ cup butter or margarine,
  softened
1 cup finely chopped pecans

Combine 2 cups sugar and whipping cream in a medium saucepan; cook over low heat, stirring frequently, until sugar dissolves. Remove from heat, and set aside.

Place remaining 1 cup sugar in a 9-inch cast-iron skillet; cook over medium heat, stirring constantly, until sugar dissolves and becomes a golden syrup. Add butter, stirring well.

Gradually pour syrup mixture into reserved cream mixture in saucepan. Cook over medium heat, stirring constantly, until mixture reaches soft ball stage (240°).

Remove from heat, and beat mixture at medium speed of electric mixer 5 minutes or until thick enough to spread. Spread immediately on cooled cake. Yield: enough frosting for one 2-layer cake.

A day at Neshoba County Fair, photographed c.1955.

DEEP SOUTH FISH FRY

Nearly any occasion can be celebrated with a fish fry, and most frequently in the South, the choice for the fish will be catfish.

Years ago, people gathered for cane grindings in Northern Florida. It was hard labor, feeding cane into the mill and boiling down the syrup, but there was a treat to look forward to. When the work was done, catfish and hush puppies were fried in an iron pot over the fire. Satisfying eating it was then... and still is today.

OGEECHEE RIVER FRIED FISH
GEORGIA CATFISH STEW
HUSH PUPPIES
PAPRIKA DRESSING WITH MIXED FRESH
SUMMER VEGETABLES
FRESH SLICED PEACHES
OLD-FASHIONED TEA CAKES

Serves 8

OGEECHEE RIVER FRIED FISH

2½ to 3 pounds catfish fillets
1 teaspoon salt
2 cups buttermilk
2 cups self-rising cornmeal
1 cup self-rising flour
Lemon quarters (optional)

Place fish in a shallow pan, and sprinkle with salt. Pour buttermilk over top, and refrigerate 30 minutes.

Combine cornmeal and flour; mix well. Remove fish from buttermilk. Dredge fish in cornmeal mixture. Carefully drop fish into deep hot oil (370°). Fry until fish float to the top and are golden brown; drain well. Serve hot. Garnish with lemon quarters, if desired. Yield: 8 servings.

Ogeechee River Fried Fish served with Hush Puppies. You just can't get better Southern food than a mess of catfish like this one.

GEORGIA CATFISH STEW

2 pounds catfish fillets
3 cups water
1½ teaspoons salt, divided
1 pound thick sliced bacon,
  cut into 1-inch pieces
4 medium potatoes, peeled
  and cut into ½-inch slices
2 medium onions, thinly
  sliced, divided
2 (14½-ounce) cans stewed
  tomatoes, drained, divided
¼ teaspoon pepper, divided
2 tablespoons sugar
3 pickled banana peppers
2 tablespoons pickled banana
  pepper juice

Place catfish in a 13- x 9- x 2-inch baking dish; add water and 1 teaspoon salt. Cover with foil; bake at 350° for 30 minutes or until fish is tender. Remove fish, reserving liquid. Let fish cool. Remove fish in large pieces from bone.

Line bottom of a large stock pot with half each of the bacon, sliced potatoes, onion, fish, and tomatoes. Sprinkle with ¼ teaspoon salt and ⅛ teaspoon pepper. Repeat layers.

Pour reserved catfish liquid over layered ingredients. Sprinkle with sugar. Place banana peppers on top; add pepper juice. Cover; bring to a boil. Reduce heat; simmer 2 to 3 hours. Do not stir. Yield: 8 servings.

HUSH PUPPIES

2 cups self-rising cornmeal
2 tablespoons self-rising flour
2 teaspoons sugar
½ teaspoon garlic powder
½ cup chopped onion
1½ cups buttermilk
2 eggs, slightly beaten

Combine first 5 ingredients; add buttermilk and eggs, stirring well.

Carefully drop batter by tablespoonfuls into deep hot oil (370°); cook only a few at a time, turning once. Fry 3 minutes or until hush puppies are golden brown. Drain well on paper towels. Yield: about 3 dozen.

Farm family waits for the fish to fry over a campfire along the banks of the Cane River, Natchitoches, Louisiana, c.1940.

Library of Congress

PAPRIKA DRESSING

1 cup mayonnaise
3 cloves garlic
2 tablespoons catsup
1 teaspoon paprika
1 teaspoon pepper
1 teaspoon dry mustard
1 teaspoon onion juice
1 teaspoon Worcestershire
  sauce
½ teaspoon prepared
  horseradish
1 teaspoon water
¼ teaspoon salt
Juice of 1 lemon
Dash of hot sauce
½ cup vegetable oil

Combine all ingredients except oil in container of electric blender; blend 5 seconds. Blend 5 more seconds, slowly adding oil. Chill; serve over mixed summer vegetables. Yield: 2 cups.

OLD-FASHIONED TEA CAKES

1 cup lard
2 cups sugar
2 eggs
1 teaspoon baking powder
½ teaspoon baking soda
½ cup buttermilk
1 teaspoon vanilla extract
About 6 cups all-purpose flour

Combine lard and sugar; beat well. Add eggs, beating well.

Dissolve baking powder and soda in buttermilk; stir well. Add to creamed mixture, mixing well. Stir in vanilla. Gradually add enough flour to make a moderately stiff dough. Divide dough in half, and chill at least 20 minutes.

Roll dough to ½-inch thickness on a lightly floured surface; cut with a 3-inch cookie cutter. Place on lightly greased baking sheets. Bake at 375° for 15 minutes or until edges are lightly browned; transfer to wire racks, and let cool completely. Yield: 1½ dozen.

CRAB FEAST ASHORE

A menu with crabmeat prepared in two ways and eaten at the seaside? A landlocked seafood lover would mortgage his house and lot for an invitation to that outing! Labor Day or any day, Marylanders and others around the Chesapeake can be seen spreading newspapers on tables and icing down beer, ready to start cracking crabs. If that heady aroma in the air is salty, peppery, and spicy, it is probably the "Old Bay" seasoning in the crab pot. A whole gen-eration has grown up on the tangy flavoring developed by Gustav C. Brunn, who came to Baltimore from Germany in 1939. He had worked in the spice business in Germany, and now he adapted himself and his season-ing to his new environment.

The exact recipe is a Brunn family secret — but it does contain a blend of the follow-ing spices: celery salt, pepper, mustard, pi-miento, cloves, laurel leaves, mace, cardamom, ginger, and paprika.

STEAMED CRABS
MARYLAND CRAB CAKES
ROASTED CORN IN THE HUSK
SLICED TOMATOES * MUSTARD PICKLE
CARAWAY ROLLS
FRESH PEACH PIE
COLD BEER

Serves 6

STEAMED CRABS

¼ cup plus 1 tablespoon Old
  Bay Seasoning
¼ cup salt
1 tablespoon pepper
Water
Vinegar
2 dozen live blue crabs

Combine Old Bay Seasoning, salt, and pepper; stir well, and set aside.

Combine equal parts of water and vinegar in a large stock pot with a steaming rack to a level just below the rack. Bring water-vinegar mixture to a boil. Add a layer of crabs; sprinkle with seasoning mixture. Repeat layers. Cover and steam 20 min-utes or until crabs turn red in color. Drain, and serve the crabs immediately. Yield: 6 servings.

MARYLAND CRAB CAKES

3 slices bread, torn into
  bite-size pieces
2 tablespoons water
1½ pounds fresh lump
  crabmeat, drained and
  flaked
2 eggs, beaten
1½ tablespoons
  mayonnaise
1½ tablespoons
  Worcestershire sauce
1½ tablespoons chopped
  fresh parsley
1½ teaspoons prepared
  mustard
1½ teaspoons Old Bay
  Seasoning
¼ teaspoon salt
Vegetable oil
Lemon wedges
Tartar sauce

Place bread in a large bowl; sprinkle with water to moisten. Add crabmeat, eggs, mayon-naise, Worcestershire sauce, chopped parsley, mustard, Old Bay Seasoning, and salt; stir well. Shape mixture into twelve 4-inch patties.

Heat ¼ inch of oil in a large skillet over medium-high heat. Cook patties 3 minutes on each side or until golden brown, turning once. Drain well on paper towels. Serve with lemon wedges and tartar sauce. Yield: 12 (4-inch) cakes.

ROASTED CORN IN THE HUSK

6 ears fresh corn
Butter or margarine
Salt and pepper to taste

Remove outer husks from corn; turn back inner husks, and remove silk. Replace inner husks over cob and tie. Let stand in cold water 1 hour. Re-move from water and drain.

Place corn on grill. Cover and cook over medium coals 30 min-utes or until corn is tender, turning ears frequently. Remove husks; serve with butter and seasonings. Yield: 6 servings.

CARAWAY ROLLS

1 package dry yeast
¾ cup warm water (105°
    to 115°)
¼ cup molasses
1 tablespoon sugar
1 tablespoon vegetable oil
2 teaspoons salt
2 teaspoons caraway seeds
1 teaspoon anise seeds
1 cup whole wheat flour
1½ to 2 cups sifted
    all-purpose flour
Crushed sea salt

Dissolve yeast in warm water in a large bowl; let stand 5 minutes or until bubbly. Add molasses, sugar, oil, 2 teaspoons salt, and caraway and anise seeds; mix well. Stir in whole wheat flour and enough all-purpose flour to make a soft dough.

Turn dough out onto a lightly floured surface. Knead dough 8 minutes or until smooth and elastic. Place in a well-greased bowl, turning to grease top. Cover and let rise in a warm place (85°), free from drafts, 1½ hours or until dough is doubled in bulk.

Punch dough down; turn out onto a lightly floured surface, and knead 4 to 5 times. Roll dough into a ¼-inch-thick circle on a lightly floured surface; cut into 12 wedges. Roll up each wedge tightly, beginning at the wide end. Seal points, and place on a lightly greased baking sheet.

Cover and repeat rising procedure 30 minutes or until doubled in bulk. Brush rolls with water, and sprinkle with crushed sea salt. Bake at 425° for 10 minutes or until browned. Yield: 1 dozen.

Steamed Crabs, Maryland Crab Cakes, and Roasted Corn.

FRESH PEACH PIE

6 cups sliced fresh peaches,
    divided
1 cup sugar
3 tablespoons cornstarch
½ cup orange juice
2 tablespoons lemon juice
1 baked 9-inch pastry shell

Mash 2 cups sliced peaches; set aside.

Combine sugar and cornstarch in a heavy saucepan; stir well. Gradually add orange juice and mashed peaches. Cook over medium heat, stirring constantly, 8 minutes or until mixture thickens. Remove from heat; stir in lemon juice. Cool glaze completely.

Brush glaze over bottom and sides of baked pastry shell, coating well. Using remaining 4 cups peaches, place a layer of peaches in pastry shell. Brush with glaze. Repeat layers, ending with glaze, completely coating peaches. Refrigerate at least 3 hours. Yield: one 9-inch pie.

Halloween

The night before All Saints' Day on November 1, we celebrate Halloween or All Hallows' Eve. Falling at the same time as the Druids' autumn festival of Samhain on the last day of October, the Christian observance naturally became mixed with the ancient pre-Christian British customs. The Druid priests worshiped nature and performed mystic ceremonies to the great sun god. (The great stone pillars around which they marched can still be seen at Stonehenge in England.) The Druidist knew that the souls of the dead returned during the autumn festival to warm themselves at their old hearths; that was acceptable. But there were also evil spirits abroad, and great bonfires were built on hilltops to honor the sun god and to keep the evil spirits at bay. After the bonfires were lit, the villagers donned masks and sang and danced around the flames, pretending to be pursued by evil spirits.

Americans paid little attention to Halloween until the Irish came here in the 1800s. They knew of an Irishman named Jack who used to play tricks on the devil and was condemned to wander forever, carrying a lantern. They found the American pumpkin made a perfect Jack o' lantern, and it became our main symbol of Halloween.

Elements of the modern Halloween can be traced to the Romans who took England: they had already integrated All Saints' Day with the festival of Pomona, goddess of fruits. We drink cider, use fruits for centerpieces, apples for bobbing and candying, and nuts symbolic of food stored for winter.

Certainly, safety measures are in order for this holiday, but these have led to a plus—now we can have parties at home.

Bewitching, benign greeting card proffered in 1909.

JOLLY HALLOW E'EN

May the fates be good to you.

BONFIRE SUPPER

A Halloween bonfire is doubly useful. The first high flame frightens away any evil spirits infesting the area. After it subsides a little, there is the heat needed for cooking burgers and steak on sticks. Foil-wrapped potatoes may be cooked in coals raked to one side. Or any of the above may be cooked on a grill. But roasted marshmallows are at their best as bonfire food! After the meal, it is customary to gather around the fire to tell—and to shudder at—ghost and goblin stories.

BONFIRE BURGERS
or
STEAK ON A STICK
CAMPFIRE ROASTED POTATOES
FRESH APPLES IN A BASKET
PUMPKIN CAKE
ROASTED MARSHMALLOWS

Serves 8

BONFIRE BURGERS

2 pounds ground beef
2 eggs, beaten
¼ cup catsup
2 tablespoons Worcestershire
  sauce
2 tablespoons finely chopped
  onion
2 teaspoons salt
8 slices bacon
8 hamburger buns,
  split and toasted
8 lettuce leaves
8 slices onion
8 slices tomato

Combine first 6 ingredients; mix well. Shape into 8 patties. Wrap a slice of bacon around each patty, securing with a wooden pick. Grill patties over medium coals 8 to 10 minutes on each side or until desired degree of doneness.

Place patties on bottom of buns. Top each with lettuce leaf and onion and tomato slices; cover with bun tops. Yield: 8 servings.

Placed on the shed roof, with candles to cast an eerie light, Jack o'lanterns will scare away the ghosts and goblins. Boys are ready for Halloween.

Brown Brothers

Bonfire fare: Steak on a Stick and Marshmallows.

PUMPKIN CAKE

1 cup shortening
3 cups sugar
3 eggs, beaten
1 (16-ounce) can pumpkin
1 teaspoon vanilla extract
3 cups all-purpose flour
½ teaspoon baking powder
1 teaspoon baking soda
¼ teaspoon salt
1 teaspoon ground allspice
1 teaspoon ground nutmeg
1 teaspoon ground cinnamon
1 teaspoon ground cloves
Cream Cheese Glaze
Candy corn (optional)

Cream shortening in a large mixing bowl; gradually add sugar, beating well. Add eggs, pumpkin, and vanilla; mix well.

Sift together flour, baking powder, soda, salt, and spices; gradually add dry ingredients to creamed mixture, beating well after each addition.

Spoon batter into a greased and floured 10-inch tube pan. Bake at 350° for 1 hour and 15 minutes or until a wooden pick inserted in center comes out clean. Cool in pan 10 minutes; invert on wire rack to cool completely. Spoon Cream Cheese Glaze over top of cake, allowing excess to drizzle down sides. Decorate with candy corn, if desired. Yield: one 10-inch cake.

Cream Cheese Glaze:

2 tablespoons butter or
  margarine, softened
1 (3-ounce) package cream
  cheese, softened
2 tablespoons apple cider
½ teaspoon vanilla extract
2¼ cups sifted powdered
  sugar

Combine all ingredients, mixing until smooth. Yield: enough for one 10-inch cake.

STEAK ON A STICK

2 pounds boneless sirloin
  steak
½ cup sherry
2 tablespoons soy sauce
1 tablespoon red wine vinegar
1 tablespoon catsup
1 tablespoon honey
⅛ teaspoon garlic powder
Commercial toasted rolls

Trim fat from steak; cut into 36 (1½-inch) cubes. Set aside.

Combine remainder of ingredients in a large shallow dish. Add steak; cover and marinate at least 2 hours in refrigerator, turning occasionally.

Drain steak, reserving marinade. Thread steak on eight 7-inch skewers. Grill 5 minutes on each side over medium coals or until desired degree of doneness, basting with marinade. Serve with toasted rolls. Yield: 8 servings.

CAMPFIRE ROASTED POTATOES

8 medium baking potatoes
2 tablespoons butter or
  margarine, softened
Butter
Salt and pepper to taste
Commercial sour cream
  (optional)

Wash potatoes well; rub with 2 tablespoons butter. Wrap each in heavy-duty aluminum foil, shiny side in. Seal tightly.

Knock gray ash off briquets or coals in grill. Lay potatoes on coals. Cook, turning frequently, for 50 to 60 minutes. Potatoes are done when they yield to soft pressure.

Open foil; slit tops and squeeze gently. Top with butter and salt and pepper to taste. Add sour cream, if desired. Yield: 8 servings.

APPLE-BOBBING PARTY

Halloween is unique among our holidays in that it celebrates the spirit of nonsense. Bobbing for apples remains a popular Halloween game, probably because it is too much fun to drop. The splashing and undignified postures of the bobbers' art will unbend the most self-conscious party-goer. Outdoors is best; apple bobbers are notoriously messy. Once faces and hair are soaked, they don't seem to mind where the water goes. Then bring on the food.

BUTTERED POPCORN
CANDIED APPLES
JACK O'LANTERN COOKIES
BLACK CAT CUPCAKES
WITCHES' BREW

Serves 10

Bobbing for apples, but mostly clowning for camera, c.1910.

CANDIED APPLES

10 medium apples
10 wooden skewers or sticks
6 cups sugar
1½ cups water
1 cup light corn syrup
2 teaspoons cinnamon extract
¼ teaspoon red food coloring

Wash and dry apples; remove stems. Insert wooden skewers into stem end of each apple. Set aside at room temperature.

Combine sugar, water, syrup, and cinnamon extract in a heavy saucepan; stir well. Bring to a boil; cover and cook 3 minutes. Uncover and continue cooking, without stirring, until mixture reaches soft crack stage (290°). Add food coloring, mixing well.

Transfer syrup to top of a double boiler. Place over boiling water, and quickly dip apples in syrup; allow excess to drip off. Place apples on lightly greased baking sheets to cool. To store, wrap tightly in plastic wrap. Yield: 10 servings.

JACK O'LANTERN COOKIES

2 eggs
2 cups sugar
¾ cup butter, melted
3½ cups all-purpose flour
2 tablespoons baking powder
½ teaspoon salt
1 teaspoon ground ginger
½ teaspoon ground cinnamon
2 tablespoons water
1 teaspoon vanilla extract
1½ cups finely chopped pecans
Frosting (recipe follows)
8 (1-ounce) squares semisweet chocolate, melted

Combine eggs, sugar, and butter in a medium mixing bowl; beat well. Combine flour, baking powder, salt, and spices. Gradually add flour mixture to egg mixture; mix well. Stir in water, vanilla, and pecans.

Divide dough into fourths; wrap in foil, and chill at least 2 hours. Roll 1 portion to ⅛-inch thickness on a well-floured surface; keep remaining dough chilled until ready to roll.

Cut dough into 3-inch circles. Place on lightly greased baking sheets. Bake at 375° for 8 minutes or until lightly browned. Remove immediately to wire rack to cool. Repeat with remaining dough. Decorate with frosting and melted chocolate. Yield: about 2½ dozen.

Frosting:

3 tablespoons butter, softened
¼ cup plus 1½ teaspoons whipping cream
⅛ teaspoon salt
3¾ cups sifted powdered sugar
1½ teaspoons vanilla extract
Orange paste food coloring

Combine butter, whipping cream, and salt; beat well. Gradually add sugar, beating until well blended. Stir in vanilla. Color small amounts of frosting with paste food coloring as needed during decorating. Decorate cookies with frosting, and pipe melted chocolate to make faces. Yield: about 2 cups.

Note: Frosting dries quickly; keep covered at all times with a damp cloth.

BLACK CAT CUPCAKES

¼ cup butter or margarine
⅔ cup sugar
1 egg, beaten
1 cup plus 2 tablespoons all-purpose flour
1¼ teaspoons baking powder
½ teaspoon salt
½ cup plus 1 tablespoon milk
1 teaspoon vanilla extract
1 cup semisweet chocolate morsels
Cocoa Cream Frosting
Gumdrops (optional)
Candy corn (optional)
Licorice ropes (optional)

Cream butter; gradually add sugar, beating well. Add egg; beat well.

Combine flour, baking powder, and salt; add to creamed mixture, alternately with milk, beginning and ending with flour mixture. Stir in vanilla and chocolate morsels.

Spoon batter into a paper-lined muffin pan, filling one-half full. Bake at 350° for 25 minutes or until lightly browned. Cool in pan 10 minutes; remove to wire rack to complete cooling. Frost with Cocoa Cream Frosting. Garnish with gumdrops, candy corn, and licorice ropes, if desired. Yield: 1 dozen.

Cocoa Cream Frosting:

¾ cup butter or margarine, softened
2¼ cups sifted powdered sugar, divided
3 tablespoons cocoa
1 teaspoon vanilla extract

Combine butter, ½ cup sugar, cocoa, and vanilla; beat at medium speed of an electric mixer until light and fluffy. Add remaining sugar, beating until smooth enough to spread. Yield: enough for 1 dozen cupcakes.

WITCHES' BREW

2 quarts apple cider
¼ cup lemon juice
⅔ cup firmly packed brown sugar
½ teaspoon ground allspice
½ teaspoon ground nutmeg
¼ teaspoon salt
12 whole cloves
2 (3-inch) sticks cinnamon

Combine first 6 ingredients in a Dutch oven. Cook over medium-high heat, stirring occasionally to dissolve sugar.

Place cloves and cinnamon on cheesecloth. Bring edges of cheesecloth together at top and tie securely to form a small bag. Drop spice bag into simmering cider mixture; continue to simmer 10 minutes, stirring occasionally. Remove spice bag; pour cider into a heat-proof punch bowl. Yield: about 2 quarts.

Halloween treats for the discerning goblin.

Day of the Hunt

W hen Robert Brooke came to Maryland in 1650, he brought along his family, his retinue of servants, and his hunting dogs. The English tradition of the hunt became a major preoccupation among the gentry of the Tidewater. George Washington left written accounts of some of the hunts he attended, as in these entries from his March, 1773 diary:

"28 Went with Mr. Dulaney and Mr. Digges, & ca., to dine with Mr. Benj. Dulaney at Mrs. French's.—

"29 Went a hunting with those Gentlemen. Found a Fox by Thos. Bailey's and had it killd by Our Dogs in half an hour.

"30 Went a hunting again—found Nothing.

In order to reassure anyone who might think that the fox is endangered, killing is no longer customary.

Fashionably dressed guests gather for a Hunt Breakfast in Richmond, 1906.

THE STIRRUP CUP

The rituals of the hunt were transported by those who came west from the coast into Tennessee and Kentucky, where they continue to be practiced by those who still thrill to the chase. There is no more colorful assemblage to be seen in the South than a group gathered for the hunt, talking a lot, eating a little, taking a bracing drink. The bright plumage is worn by the men. If a Kentuckian sports a "pink" coat, it means that he has been a working member of the club for a year and has received the buttons for his green vest. Up until that time, he has worn black. The horses are of many kinds: quarter horses make good hunters, as do Appaloosas. Standardbreds and thoroughbreds are rare in hunting circles. The Stirrup Cup is only a sip and a bite, for the dogs are wild with anticipation, the horses eager to begin.

TINY CHEDDAR BISCUITS
GLAZED BREAD BOWS
COFFEE WITH BRANDY
SPICED TEA

Serves 12

TINY CHEDDAR BISCUITS

1 cup plus 2 tablespoons
  all-purpose flour
¼ teaspoon salt
⅛ teaspoon red pepper
½ cup butter or margarine,
  softened
1 cup (4 ounces) shredded
  sharp Cheddar cheese
¼ cup milk
Pecan halves

Combine flour, salt, and pepper; cut in butter and cheese until mixture resembles coarse meal. Add milk; stir until ingredients are moistened. Turn dough out onto a floured surface; knead 3 to 4 times.

Shape dough into a 12-inch roll, about 1½-inches in diameter; wrap in waxed paper, and chill 2 to 3 hours or until firm.

Unwrap roll, and cut into ½-inch slices. Place on lightly greased baking sheets; press a pecan half in the center of each. Bake at 350° for 20 minutes. Let cool slightly on baking sheets. Remove to wire racks to cool completely. Yield: 2 dozen.

The Stirrup Cup, Sherwood Forest plantation.

Fox Chase, subtitled Throwing Off, *lithograph by N. Currier, 1846.*

GLAZED BREAD BOWS

3 to 3¼ cups all-purpose
  flour, divided
1 package dry yeast
¼ cup sugar
1 teaspoon salt
½ cup milk
⅓ cup butter or margarine
2 eggs
½ teaspoon lemon extract
2 cups sifted powdered sugar
2 tablespoons lemon juice

Combine 1 cup flour, yeast, ¼ cup sugar, and salt in a large mixing bowl; set aside.

Combine milk and butter in a small saucepan; heat to 120° to 130°, stirring well. Add to flour mixture. Add eggs and lemon extract; beat at medium speed of electric mixer 3 minutes. Stir in enough remaining flour to make a soft dough.

Shape dough into a ball. Place in a greased bowl, turning to grease top. Cover and let rise in a warm place (85°), free from drafts, 1 hour or until doubled in bulk.

Punch dough down. Repeat rising procedure 45 minutes or until doubled in bulk.

Punch dough down. Turn dough out onto a floured surface; let rest 5 minutes. Roll dough into a 12-inch square. Cut into 4- x 1-inch strips. Twist ends of each strip in opposite directions. Slightly stretch each strip, and tie into a loose knot. Place on greased baking sheets.

Cover and repeat rising procedure 45 minutes or until doubled in bulk. Bake at 375° for 10 minutes or until golden brown. Combine powdered sugar and lemon juice; mix well, and drizzle over bows. Yield: 3 dozen.

SPICED TEA

2 medium lemons
1½ teaspoons whole
  cloves
7 cup-size tea bags
2 teaspoons whole cloves
2 teaspoons whole allspice
10⅔ cups boiling water
2 cups sugar
1⅓ cups orange juice
⅔ cup lemon juice

Cut each lemon into 6 slices; stud slices with 1½ teaspoons cloves; set aside.

Combine tea bags and remaining spices in a large Dutch oven. Pour boiling water into Dutch oven. Cover and let steep 15 minutes. Remove tea bags and spices. Add sugar and orange and lemon juice. Pour tea mixture into a heat-proof punch bowl. Add clove-studded lemon slices. Serve hot. Yield: about 3 quarts.

THE HUNT BREAKFAST

The oldest hunt club in Kentucky is the Iroquois Hounds of Lexington. Long Run Hounds of Louisville began around 1960, under Master of Hounds Judge R. R. Dalton. A Joint Master was added soon after the club's founding. The Hunt Breakfast at Long Run was (and still is) a feast, and Judge Dalton was called upon each year to act as master of ceremonies. His wit, it is said, was incomparable and his fondness for bourbon and "branch" heroic. At his death, his son, Stuart, became Joint Master.

"Cubbing" (training sessions for the dogs) starts in September, but the hunting season proper lasts from November to March.

FRIED COUNTRY HAM
JO'S EGG CASSEROLE
SOUTHERN "ICE CREAM" GRITS
CURRIED FRUIT
FOOLPROOF BISCUITS
CHOCOLATE PIE
BOURBON AND BRANCH WATER

Serves 12

FRIED COUNTRY HAM

**12 (¼-inch-thick) slices
center-cut country ham**

Trim fat from ham slices, leaving ¼ inch fat remaining. Score fat at 1-inch intervals to prevent curling.

Preheat electric skillet to low (225°); place first ham slice in skillet, fat side of ham near edge of pan.

Place second slice on top of first, with fat side of ham near opposite edge of pan.

Stack remaining ham slices overlapping each slice so fat side is near edge of pan.

Cover skillet, and cook over low heat 15 minutes. Remove ham slices from skillet. Turn over each slice, and return slices to skillet, repeating stacking procedure.

Cover and continue cooking an additional 10 minutes. Yield: 12 servings.

Favor of the Hunt, from the American Historical Series by J. L. G. Ferris. The custom, long obsolete, was to bring back the tail or "brush" of the fox.

Archives of 76, Bay Village, Ohio

JO'S EGG CASSEROLE

2 pounds bulk Italian
   sausage
9 slices bread
¾ teaspoon dry mustard
9 eggs, beaten
1 (4½-ounce) jar sliced
   mushrooms, drained
1½ cups (6 ounces) shredded
   sharp Cheddar cheese
3 cups milk

Cook sausage until browned, stirring to crumble; drain well. Place sausage in a lightly greased 13- x 9- x 2-inch baking dish or two 1½-quart casseroles, if desired.

Remove crust from bread; cut bread into cubes. Combine bread cubes and remaining ingredients; mixing well. Pour mixture over sausage; cover and refrigerate overnight.

Bake, covered, at 350° for 30 minutes. Uncover and bake an additional 30 minutes. Yield: 12 servings.

SOUTHERN "ICE CREAM" GRITS

3 cups milk
3 cups water
1 teaspoon salt
2 cups uncooked regular
   grits
½ cup butter or margarine
3 cups (12 ounces) shredded
   sharp Cheddar cheese
2 tablespoons grated
   Parmesan cheese
1 teaspoon paprika

Combine milk, water, and salt in a medium saucepan; bring to a boil over medium heat. Add grits, stirring well. Reduce heat; cover and cook 10 minutes, stirring occasionally. Add butter and Cheddar cheese; stir until melted. Cool 10 minutes.

Scoop grits into a serving bowl using an ice cream scoop. Combine Parmesan cheese and paprika; mix well. Sprinkle cheese mixture over tops of scoops just before serving. Yield: 12 servings.

CURRIED FRUIT

2 (17-ounce) cans apricot
   halves
1 (16-ounce) can pineapple
   slices, halved
1 (29-ounce) can peach halves
1 (17-ounce) can figs
1 (6-ounce) jar maraschino
   cherries
1 cup firmly packed light
   brown sugar
¼ cup butter or margarine
1½ teaspoons curry powder

Drain all fruit, reserving ½ cup each of apricot and pineapple juice. Set juice aside.

Place drained fruit in a 12- x 8- x 2-inch baking dish, and set aside.

Combine reserved juice, sugar, butter, and curry powder in a medium saucepan. Bring to a boil. Reduce heat, and simmer 30 minutes or until syrup thickens. Pour syrup over fruit. Bake, uncovered, at 350° for 20 minutes. Spoon fruit into serving dish using a slotted spoon. Yield: 12 servings.

FOOLPROOF BISCUITS

4 cups self-rising flour
2 teaspoons baking powder
½ cup shortening
1½ cups milk

Combine flour and baking powder; stir well. Cut in shortening until mixture resembles coarse meal. Sprinkle milk evenly over flour mixture, stirring just until dry ingredients are moistened.

Turn dough out onto a lightly floured surface; knead lightly 10 to 12 times.

Roll dough to ½-inch thickness; cut with a 2½-inch biscuit cutter. Place biscuits on greased baking sheets. Bake at 425° for 12 minutes or until lightly browned. Yield: about 2 dozen.

CHOCOLATE PIE

1½ cups sugar
3 tablespoons cocoa
3 tablespoons all-purpose
   flour
Dash of salt
1 egg, beaten
3 eggs, separated
1½ cups boiling water
1½ teaspoons vanilla extract
1 baked 9-inch pastry shell
¼ cup plus 2 tablespoons
   sugar
Shaved chocolate

Mix 1½ cups sugar, cocoa, flour, and salt in a large saucepan. Stir in 1 egg; beat 3 egg yolks and add to cocoa mixture, mixing well. Pour boiling water over cocoa mixture, stirring constantly. Cook and stir over medium heat for 5 to 10 minutes or until mixture thickens. Remove from heat and add vanilla. Pour into pastry shell.

Beat 3 egg whites until foamy in a small mixing bowl. Add remaining sugar gradually, beating until mixture forms stiff peaks. Spoon on top of pie; bake at 350° for 10 minutes or until meringue is browned. Sprinkle top with shaved chocolate. Yield: one 9-inch pie.

Note: Meringue may be omitted and whipped cream used as topping instead.

Fried Country Ham, Curried Fruit, Southern "Ice Cream" Grits, Foolproof Biscuits, and Jo's Egg Casserole. "Bourbon and Branch" is the proper Hunt Breakfast drink.

Thanksgiving

The harvest or Thanksgiving dinner on the following pages reflects foods whose existence in colonial times has been verified through sources such as gardening records and rare books at the colonial Williamsburg Research Center, and John Smith's 1624 *Generall Historie of Virginia*. The recipes are delicious and will certainly make for an authentic celebration. That said, it might be worthwhile to go looking for the origins of Thanksgiving. "Ah," you say. "The old New England Pilgrims again."

Not according to Samuel Eliot Morison, famed New England historian: "The Pilgrims never had a regular fall Thanksgiving day. More bunk has been written about Pilgrims than any other subject except Columbus and John Paul Jones, not even excepting the Civil War."

According to myth, the first "Thanksgiving" took place when a boatload of pious Pilgrims held a European-style harvest celebration at Plymouth in 1621. Fully a decade before the Pilgrims got their first festival together, several "thanksgivings" had already been celebrated in Virginia, but they were unofficial and purely religious in nature. The most touching of these services took place in June of 1610. Of the 490 colonists inhabiting Jamestown at the onset of winter, only six pathetic souls survived the "starving time" to get on their knees and give thanks for the gift of life.

Now for Thanksgiving with a capital T. Captain John Woodleaf and his 38 men, two and a half months out of Bristol, landed on the banks of the James River at the Berkeley Hundred on December 4, 1619. (December 14 by the "new-style" calendar we adopted in 1752.) Captain Woodleaf decreed, ". . . the day of our ships arrival at the place assigned for plantacon in the land of Virginia shall be yearly and perpetually kept holy as a day of thanksgiving to Almighty God." And that places Virginia as the one and only site of the first official Thanksgiving in America, over a year before the Pilgrims made landfall hundreds of miles to the North.

Welcome Thanksgiving

Busy hands
make
a happy heart,
May Health
and
Wealth
their share
impart.

In 1963, President John F. Kennedy issued a proclamation confirming what Virginians had known all along: The first Thanksgiving was held at Berkeley on the banks of the James River. To commemorate this event there is an annual Thanksgiving Festival held at Berkeley on an early Sunday in November; the public is invited.

THANKSGIVING ON THE EAST COAST

Thanksgiving, like Christmas, is a time of reunion, an ingathering of family and friends as well as the harvest. There is a tradition in some Southern churches that brings members together into an enlarged family for a Thanksgiving celebration. One is the All Hallows Church in Davidsonville, Maryland.

An East coast holiday meal without oysters would be unthinkable, and the women of the church know, as their grandmothers knew, that the turkeys must be not only locally born and bred, but also freshly killed and dressed.

ROAST TURKEY
SAGE DRESSING WITH GIBLET GRAVY
CRANBERRY FRAPPÉ
CREAMED ONIONS
SAVANNAH BAKED OYSTERS
SOUTHERN CORN PUDDING
BRUSSELS SPROUTS WITH DILL BUTTER
CRABAPPLES * OLIVES * SWEET PICKLES
CELERY VASE
SWEET POTATO MUFFINS
FIG PUDDING
MARYLAND WHITE POTATO PIE
BERKELEY SPICED CIDER

Serves 12

ROAST TURKEY

1 (10- to 12-pound) turkey
2 teaspoons salt
2 teaspoons pepper
¼ cup butter or margarine, melted

Remove giblets and neck from turkey; reserve for Giblet Gravy, if desired. Rinse turkey thoroughly with cold water; pat dry. Combine salt and pepper; sprinkle over surface and in cavity of turkey.

Close cavity of turkey with skewers. Tie ends of legs to tail with string or tuck them under flap of skin around tail. Lift wingtips up and over back, tucking under bird securely.

Brush entire bird with melted butter; place turkey, breast side up, on a rack in roasting pan. Insert meat thermometer in breast or meaty part of thigh, making sure thermometer does not touch bone. Bake at 325° for 4½ to 5 hours or until meat thermometer registers 185°.

Baste turkey frequently with pan drippings. If turkey gets too brown, cover lightly with aluminum foil.

When turkey is two-thirds done, cut the cord or band of skin holding the drumstick ends to the tail; this will ensure that the insides of the thighs are cooked. Turkey is done when drumsticks are easy to move.

Transfer turkey to serving platter. Let stand 15 minutes before carving. Yield: 12 to 16 servings.

Note: Leftover turkey may be refrigerated for later use.

SAGE DRESSING WITH GIBLET GRAVY

1 cup finely chopped celery
¾ cup finely chopped onion
1 cup water
6 cups cornbread crumbs
4 cups soft breadcrumbs
½ cup butter or margarine, softened
¼ teaspoon rubbed sage
1 tablespoon salt
⅛ teaspoon pepper
4 eggs, beaten
2¼ cups chicken or turkey broth
Giblet Gravy

Cook celery and onion in water over low heat until tender; drain. Combine cooked vegetables, cornbread crumbs, breadcrumbs, butter, sage, salt, and pepper in a large bowl; mix well. Add eggs and broth, stirring until well blended.

Spoon dressing into a lightly greased 13- x 9- x 2-inch baking dish. Bake at 400° for 30 minutes or until lightly browned. Cut dressing into squares, and serve with Giblet Gravy. Yield: 12 servings.

Giblet Gravy:

¼ cup pan drippings from turkey or chicken
¼ cup all-purpose flour
1½ cups turkey or chicken broth
½ cup milk
¼ cup chopped cooked giblets
2 hard-cooked eggs, chopped
¼ teaspoon salt
⅛ teaspoon pepper

Heat pan drippings in a large skillet over low heat. Add flour, stirring until smooth. Cook 1 minute, stirring constantly. Gradually add broth and milk; cook over medium heat, stirring constantly, until thickened and bubbly. Add giblets, eggs, salt, and pepper, stirring well. Yield: about 2 cups.

CRANBERRY FRAPPÉ

2 cups fresh cranberries
2 cups water
2 cups boiling water
3 oranges, halved
3 lemons, halved
2 cups sugar

Combine cranberries and water in a medium saucepan. Bring to a boil. Reduce heat; cover and simmer 20 minutes or until cranberries are soft. Strain cranberries, reserving liquid. Press pulp through strainer; discard seeds and skins. Combine strained pulp and liquid. Set aside.

Pour boiling water over orange and lemon halves; let stand 20 minutes. Remove oranges and lemons, reserving water. Juice oranges and lemons; strain juice, and add to cranberry pulp mixture. Remove pulp from orange and lemon halves, reserving shells. Add reserved water and sugar to cranberry mixture; stir well.

Fill reserved orange and lemon shells with cranberry mixture; freeze until firm. Pour remaining cranberry mixture into a 9- x 5- x 3-inch loafpan; cover and freeze until firm. Use filled orange and lemon shells as a garnish for meat dishes, if desired. Remaining frappé may be scooped into individual serving dishes. Yield: 2 quarts.

CREAMED ONIONS

7 medium onions, thinly sliced
¾ cup butter or margarine
3 tablespoons all-purpose flour
1½ teaspoons salt
¼ teaspoon dry mustard
⅛ teaspoon white pepper
1½ cups milk

Sauté onion slices in butter in a large heavy skillet until tender. Add flour, salt, mustard, and pepper, stirring until a smooth paste is formed. Gradually add milk; cook over medium heat, stirring frequently, until thickened. Yield: 12 servings.

SAVANNAH BAKED OYSTERS

1 cup finely chopped celery
¼ cup butter or margarine
4 cups herb-seasoned stuffing mix
1 cup finely chopped fresh parsley
1 teaspoon salt
¼ teaspoon pepper
6 (12-ounce) containers fresh Select oysters, drained
½ cup butter, melted

Sauté celery in ¼ cup butter until tender.

Combine stuffing mix, parsley, sautéed celery, salt, and pepper; stir well.

Layer half of oysters in a lightly greased 12- x 8- x 2-inch baking dish; top with half of stuffing mixture. Repeat layers; pour remaining butter over mixture in baking dish. Bake at 350° for 30 minutes or until bubbly. Yield: 12 servings.

SOUTHERN CORN PUDDING

6 eggs
3 cups milk
6 cups fresh corn, cut from cob
¼ cup plus 2 tablespoons butter or margarine, melted
¼ cup sugar
¼ cup all-purpose flour
½ teaspoon salt
¼ teaspoon pepper

Combine eggs and milk, beating well. Add remaining ingredients; stir well.

Pour into 2 greased 1½-quart casseroles. Bake at 375° for 40 minutes or until set. Yield: 12 servings.

Clockwise from front: Brussels Sprouts with Dill Butter, Sage Dressing with Giblet Gravy, pickles and olives, Sweet Potato Muffins, Celery Vase, Cranberry Frappé, and Southern Corn Pudding. Top left: Roast Turkey.

BRUSSELS SPROUTS WITH DILL BUTTER

4 (8-ounce) packages frozen
  brussels sprouts
¼ cup plus 2 tablespoons
  butter or margarine, melted
1 teaspoon dried whole
  dillweed
½ teaspoon salt
¼ teaspoon pepper
Fresh dillweed

Cook brussels sprouts according to package directions;
drain. Place in a serving dish,
and keep warm.

Combine next 4 ingredients;
pour over brussels sprouts. Garnish with fresh dillweed. Yield:
12 servings.

SWEET POTATO MUFFINS

¼ cup plus 2 tablespoons
  butter or margarine,
  softened
¾ cup sugar
1¼ cups cooked, mashed
  sweet potatoes
2 eggs
1½ cups all-purpose flour
1 tablespoon baking powder
1 teaspoon ground cinnamon
¼ teaspoon ground nutmeg
¼ teaspoon salt
1 cup milk
½ cup raisins, chopped
¼ cup chopped pecans
¼ cup sugar
½ teaspoon ground cinnamon

Cream butter; gradually add
¾ cup sugar, beating well. Add
sweet potatoes and eggs, beating well.

Combine flour, baking powder, 1 teaspoon cinnamon, nutmeg, and salt. Add flour mixture
to creamed mixture alternately
with milk, beginning and ending with flour mixture. Stir in
raisins and pecans.

Spoon batter into greased
miniature muffin pans, filling
two-thirds full. Combine ¼ cup
sugar and ½ teaspoon cinnamon; sprinkle evenly over each
muffin. Bake at 400° for 25 to 30
minutes. Yield: about 2 dozen.

FIG PUDDING

¼ cup butter or margarine,
  softened
1 cup sugar
3 eggs, beaten
½ cup sherry
1 teaspoon ground cinnamon
1 cup chopped stewed figs
2 cups stale breadcrumbs
1 cup chopped pecans
Hard Sauce

Cream butter in a large mixing bowl; gradually add sugar,
beating well. Add eggs; beat
well. Add sherry and cinnamon;
mix well. Stir in figs, breadcrumbs, and pecans.

Spoon mixture into a well-
greased 1-quart pudding mold,
and cover tightly with lid.

Place mold on a shallow rack
in a large stock pot with enough
boiling water to come halfway
up mold. Cover pot; let simmer
3 hours, replenishing water as
needed. Unmold and serve with
Hard Sauce. Store leftover pudding in refrigerator; reheat before serving. Yield: 12 servings.

Hard Sauce:

½ cup butter or margarine,
  softened
2 cups sifted powdered
  sugar
1 egg yolk, beaten
2 tablespoons brandy
½ teaspoon vanilla extract

Cream butter; gradually add
sugar, beating well. Add remaining ingredients, mixing
well. Yield: about 2 cups.

MARYLAND WHITE POTATO PIE

2¼ cups hot cooked, mashed
  potatoes
⅔ cup butter or margarine
1 cup sugar
½ teaspoon baking powder
½ teaspoon salt
⅛ teaspoon ground nutmeg
4 eggs, beaten
2 teaspoons grated lemon
  rind
2 tablespoons lemon juice
½ cup milk
½ cup whipping cream
1 teaspoon vanilla extract
1 unbaked 9-inch pastry
  shell

Combine potatoes and butter;
stir until butter melts. Add
sugar, baking powder, salt, nutmeg, eggs, lemon rind and juice,
milk, whipping cream, and vanilla; beat just until smooth.

Pour filling into pastry shell;
bake at 425° for 8 minutes. Reduce heat to 350°; bake an additional 40 minutes or until a
knife inserted in center comes
out clean. Cool pie before serving. Yield: one 9-inch pie.

BERKELEY SPICED CIDER

3 cups orange juice
¾ cup lemon juice
½ cup sugar
6 (3-inch) sticks cinnamon
1 tablespoon whole cloves
1 tablespoon ground
  nutmeg
3 quarts apple cider
½ cup applejack (optional)
Additional sticks cinnamon
  (optional)

Combine orange juice, lemon
juice, sugar, 6 sticks cinnamon,
cloves, and nutmeg in a Dutch
oven over medium heat; cook
until sugar dissolves and mixture is thoroughly heated. Add
cider, stirring well. Add applejack, if desired. Strain mixture,
discarding stick cinnamon and
cloves; pour into cups. Serve
with stick cinnamon, if desired.
Yield: about 4 quarts.

TEXAS THANKSGIVING

In the old days of the Texas cattle barons, Thanksgiving was not complete without enough wild turkeys to serve everyone connected with the ranch as well as numerous invited guests.

A Texas feast had to rely on vegetables grown on the ranch, such as red beans or pintos, cabbage, and turnips; other garden vegetables did not thrive in the hot weather and dry soil of ranch country. What did thrive was an immense hospitality, heartfelt sharing.

TEXAS ROAST TURKEY
DICED TURNIPS * RED BEANS
COMPANY SWEET POTATOES
SWEET AND SOUR SLAW
PARKERHOUSE ROLLS
BOILED CUSTARD
HOMEMADE MINCEMEAT PIE

Serves 10

Doris Lee's 1935 painting captures Thanksgiving activity in an old-time kitchen.

Courtesy of The Art Institute of Chicago

TEXAS ROAST TURKEY

1 (12-pound) turkey
2½ cups water
1 teaspoon salt
1 teaspoon pepper
4 cups cubed French bread
4 cups cornbread crumbs
1 cup chopped onion
1 cup chopped celery
3 eggs, beaten
3 tablespoons butter or
  margarine, melted
1 teaspoon salt
1 teaspoon pepper
½ teaspoon rubbed sage
¼ cup vegetable oil

Remove giblets and neck from turkey; rinse giblets and neck thoroughly, and place in a medium saucepan. Add water, and bring to a boil. Reduce heat; cover and simmer 30 minutes. Remove giblets and neck, reserving broth. Discard neck; chop giblets, and set aside.

Rinse turkey thoroughly with cold water, and pat dry. Combine 1 teaspoon salt and 1 teaspoon pepper; sprinkle in cavity of turkey.

Combine bread cubes, cornbread crumbs, onion, celery, eggs, butter, 1 teaspoon pepper, sage, reserved broth, and giblets; mix well.

Stuff dressing into cavity of turkey; close with skewers. Tie ends of legs to tail with string or tuck them under band of skin at tail. Lift wingtips up and over back, tucking under bird securely. Place turkey, breast side up, in a roasting pan.

Cover surface of turkey with several layers of cheesecloth. Brush with oil. Bake at 325° for 1 hour, basting occasionally. Remove cheesecloth; bake an additional 2½ hours or until drumsticks are easy to move. Baste occasionally with pan drippings.

Remove skewers. Transfer turkey to serving platter. Let stand at least 15 minutes before carving. Serve stuffing from turkey cavity or transfer to a serving bowl. Yield: 12 to 16 servings.

Texas Thanksgiving dinner: Texas Roast Turkey, Red Beans, Company Sweet Potatoes, and Diced Turnips.

DICED TURNIPS

6 pounds turnips, peeled and
  cubed
2 tablespoons sugar
1 teaspoon salt
¼ cup plus 2 tablespoons
  whipping cream
2 eggs, beaten
Chopped fresh parsley

Combine turnips, sugar, salt, and enough water to cover turnips; bring to a boil. Reduce heat; cover and simmer 30 minutes or until tender. Drain.

Combine cream and eggs, mixing well. Pour sauce over turnips, mixing gently. Garnish with parsley before serving. Yield: 10 servings.

RED BEANS

1½ pounds dried pinto beans
¼ pound salt pork
1 medium onion, finely
  chopped
1 clove garlic, minced
1½ teaspoons salt
¾ teaspoon chili powder

Sort and wash beans; place in a large Dutch oven. Add salt pork, onion, and garlic. Add water to cover 3 inches above beans; stir well.

Bring to a boil. Reduce heat; cover and simmer 3 hours, stirring occasionally. Uncover and continue cooking an additional 30 minutes. Stir in salt and chili powder. Yield: 10 servings.

COMPANY SWEET POTATOES

3 cups cooked, mashed
   sweet potatoes
1 cup sugar
½ cup milk
¼ cup butter or margarine,
   melted
2 eggs, beaten
1 teaspoon vanilla
   extract
1 cup flaked coconut
1 cup firmly packed
   brown sugar
⅓ cup all-purpose flour
⅓ cup butter or margarine,
   melted
1 cup chopped pecans

Combine sweet potatoes, sugar, milk, butter, eggs, and vanilla in a large bowl; mix well. Spoon into a lightly greased 2-quart casserole.

Combine coconut, brown sugar, flour, ⅓ cup melted butter, and pecans, mixing well. Sprinkle over top of sweet potatoes. Bake at 375° for 45 minutes or until golden brown. Yield: 10 servings.

SWEET AND SOUR SLAW

1 large cabbage, shredded
2 medium-size green peppers,
   sliced into rings
1 large onion, thinly sliced
   and separated into rings
2 cups vinegar
1 cup vegetable oil
1 cup water
1 cup sugar
½ teaspoon salt
⅛ teaspoon pepper

Combine cabbage, green pepper, and onion in a large bowl; mix well, and set aside.

Combine remaining ingredients; stir into cabbage mixture. Cover and chill at least 6 hours or overnight. Spoon slaw into serving plate using a slotted spoon. Yield: 10 servings.

Asking the blessing at Thanksgiving dinner, 1910.

PARKERHOUSE ROLLS

1 cup milk, scalded
3 tablespoons shortening
3 tablespoons sugar
1 teaspoon salt
1 package dry yeast
¼ cup warm water (105°
   to 115°)
1 egg, beaten
3½ cups all-purpose flour
Butter or margarine, melted

Combine scalded milk, shortening, sugar, and salt in a large mixing bowl; stir until shortening melts. Cool to lukewarm.

Dissolve yeast in warm water; let stand 5 minutes or until bubbly. Add dissolved yeast and egg to milk mixture; beat well. Stir in flour to form a soft dough.

Turn dough out onto a lightly floured surface, and knead 5 minutes or until smooth and elastic. Place in a well-greased bowl, turning to grease top. Cover and let rise in a warm place (85°), free from drafts, 2 hours or until doubled in bulk.

Punch dough down. Turn out onto a lightly floured surface, and roll to ¼-inch thickness. Cut into 2½-inch circles, and brush with melted butter.

Make a crease across each circle, and fold one half over. Gently press edges to seal. Place on greased baking sheets. Cover and repeat rising procedure 45 minutes or until doubled in bulk. Bake at 400° for 8 minutes. Yield: about 4 dozen rolls.

BOILED CUSTARD

8 eggs
1½ cups sugar
⅛ teaspoon salt
4 cups milk
2 teaspoons vanilla extract
Whipped cream

Place eggs in top of a double boiler; beat at medium speed of electric mixer until frothy. Combine sugar and salt; gradually add to eggs, beating until thick.

Bring water to a boil in bottom of a double boiler. Gradually pour milk into egg mixture, stirring constantly. Reduce heat to low; cook custard over boiling water, stirring occasionally, 20 minutes or until mixture thickens and coats a metal spoon. Stir in vanilla. Pour into serving bowls, and chill thoroughly. Garnish each serving with a dollop of whipped cream. Yield: 10 servings.

HOMEMADE MINCEMEAT PIE

2½ cups peeled, chopped
  apples
2½ cups firmly packed brown
  sugar
1 cup apple cider
1 cup raisins
½ cup currants
½ cup chopped pecans
½ cup vinegar
½ cup molasses
1½ teaspoons grated lemon
  rind
2 tablespoons lemon juice
1½ teaspoons ground
  cinnamon
1½ teaspoons ground nutmeg
1½ teaspoons ground cloves
¾ teaspoon salt
¾ teaspoon pepper
1½ pounds lean ground beef
Double-crust pastry (recipe
  follows)
2 tablespoons whipping
  cream
2 tablespoons sugar

Combine first 15 ingredients in a large Dutch oven; stir well. Cook over medium heat 15 minutes. Add beef; cook an additional 15 minutes. Cool.

Divide pastry into 4 equal portions. Roll one portion of pastry to ⅛-inch thickness, and fit into a 9-inch pieplate. Repeat procedure with a second portion of pastry.

Spoon half of mincemeat mixture into each pastry shell.

Roll third portion of pastry to ⅛-inch thickness; cut into ¾-inch wide strips, and arrange in lattice design over filling. Seal and flute edges. Brush pastry with 1 tablespoon whipping cream; sprinkle with 1 tablespoon sugar. Repeat procedure with remaining portion of pastry.

Bake pies at 350° for 55 minutes or until golden brown. Cool before serving. Yield: two 9-inch double-crust pies.

Double-Crust Pastry:

4 cups all-purpose
  flour
1 teaspoon salt
1⅓ cups shortening
½ to ¾ cup cold water

Combine flour and salt; cut in shortening with a pastry blender until mixture resembles coarse meal. Sprinkle cold water evenly over surface; stir with a fork until dry ingredients are moistened. Shape dough into a ball; chill. Yield: pastry for two 9-inch double-crust pies.

M arion Harland had this to say of mince pie: "If (it) is to deserve its name and honorable estate, it must be made at home. Nay, more, the dogma that no part of the process can be slighted without endangering the fair construction as an entirety, must be etched, and the lines well bitten in upon the domestic conscience. At least ten days before . . . clear decent space and wide, for the ceremony of mince-meat making. A sort of jocund dignity should attend preliminaries and manufacture. The kitchen must be clean and set in order . . . The middle distance should be occupied by reserves of material . . . .

Let mistress and assistants seat themselves . . . and . . . engage first of all the currants . . . ."

DON'T BE AFRAID OF HOUSEWORK, TRY TO HELP YOUR HUSBAND BY DOING YOUR OWN WORK HE WILL APPRECIATE IT.

The little woman has taken the words of this nineteenth-century advertisement to heart.

Collection of Business Americana

Merry Christmas!

Since the exact date of Christ's birth is not known, its anniversary passed without note until the middle of the fourth century A.D. when the Bishop of Rome set the date of December 25. Just as Easter was made to coincide with the existing feast of Eostre, Christmas was placed alongside the Mithraic feast of the sun god and that of the Roman Saturnalia. In addition, the Jewish feast of Hanukkah and the north European feast of the winter solstice took place at about the same time.

With so many observances already on the calendar, it made sense to wedge Christmas in because, as the Bishop doubtless hoped, Christmas gradually absorbed or displaced some of the pagan holidays. Religious first, then secular, Christmas became a period of general feasting and merrymaking, especially in England. London streets were decked with evergreens, symbolic of eternal life, and in the early 1800s Sir Walter Scott aptly described the British observance of Christmas:

> England was merry England, when
> Old Christmas brought his sports again . . .
> A Christmas gambol oft would cheer
> The poor man's heart through half the year.

Ceremonies such as the Yule Log, rooted in the old winter solstice feast, easily translated into Christmas tradition. The custom of caroling came to England with the Normans, and it was the English who composed some of our best-loved carols. Interestingly, many of the old carols would not be in existence today if they had not been preserved in the South, where Puritanism had little or no influence. The manger scenes of Christmas date back to St. Francis of Assisi and the 1200s. The Moravian "Putz" is a complex, enlarged version of the Nativity. Here is Christmas, holiest of days, with feasting Southern style.

Charming sleighful of season's greetings, dated 1900.

TREE TRIMMERS' DESSERT PARTY

Christmas was being celebrated in the North by the middle of the nineteenth century. In 1832, a Camden, Massachusetts man named Charles Follen had a lighted Christmas tree in his home, and his example was followed by others. The Germans of New Braunfels, Texas, brought their Christmas custom of a decorated cedar tree with them when they settled the area. A visitor reported seeing a tree there "decorated in the best finery of the outpost" in 1846.

Tree trimmings on the Eastern seaboard tended to reflect our British ancestory. Handmade Victorian dolls and ornaments were frequently imported and dozens of candles graced the tree — cedar, spruce, and pine were all choices.

SYLLABUB
HUGUENOT TORTE
PUMPKIN PECAN PIE
COCONUT CREAM CAKE
PINEAPPLE PECAN CAKE

Serves 12

SYLLABUB

1¼ cups sifted powdered
 sugar
½ cup plus 2 tablespoons
 white wine
3 tablespoons plus 1
 teaspoon brandy
3 tablespoons plus 1
 teaspoon grated lemon rind
2½ tablespoons lemon juice
10 cups whipping cream,
 whipped
Orange rind curls (optional)
Ground nutmeg (optional)

Combine sugar, wine, brandy, lemon rind, and juice in a large bowl; beat until well blended. Fold in whipped cream. Spoon into serving glasses.

Dip orange rind curls in nutmeg to garnish each glass, if desired. Yield: 12 servings.

Christmas desserts as once served at Middleton Place, Charleston.

HUGUENOT TORTE

2 eggs
1¼ cups sugar
¼ cup all-purpose flour,
 sifted
2½ teaspoons baking powder
¼ teaspoon salt
1 cup peeled, diced cooking
 apples
1 cup chopped pecans
1 teaspoon vanilla extract
Whipped cream

Beat eggs until thick and lemon colored; gradually add sugar, beating well. Combine flour, baking powder, and salt; add to egg mixture. Beat 1 minute at medium speed of an electric mixer. Stir in apples, pecans, and vanilla.

Pour batter into a greased 13- x 9- x 2-inch baking pan; bake at 350° for 30 minutes or until top of torte falls and becomes crusty. Let torte cool completely before cutting; cut into squares. Garnish each serving with a dollop of whipped cream. Yield: 12 servings.

PUMPKIN PECAN PIE

1 (16-ounce) can pumpkin
1¼ cups milk, scalded
1½ cups firmly packed brown
 sugar, divided
3 eggs, beaten
1 tablespoon all-purpose flour
1 teaspoon ground cinnamon
1 teaspoon ground ginger
¼ teaspoon salt
1 unbaked 9-inch pastry
 shell
¼ cup butter or margarine,
 melted
¾ cup chopped pecans

Combine pumpkin, milk, ½ cup brown sugar, eggs, flour, spices, and salt; beat 1 minute or until smooth at medium speed of an electric mixer. Pour into pastry shell; bake at 350° for 45 minutes.

Combine butter, 1 cup brown sugar, and pecans; mix well. Sprinkle pecan mixture evenly over top of pie. Reduce heat to 325°, and bake 25 minutes. Cool before serving. Yield: one 9-inch pie.

COCONUT CREAM CAKE

¾ cup shortening
1½ cups sugar
3 eggs
2¼ cups sifted cake flour
2½ teaspoons baking powder
½ teaspoon salt
¾ cup milk
1 teaspoon vanilla extract
Custard Cream Frosting
1 cup flaked coconut

Cream shortening; gradually add sugar, beating until light and fluffy. Add eggs, one at a time, beating well after each addition.

Combine flour, baking powder, and salt; add to creamed mixture alternately with milk, beginning and ending with flour mixture. Stir in vanilla.

Pour batter into 2 greased and floured 9-inch round cakepans. Bake at 375° for 25 minutes or until a wooden pick inserted in center comes out clean. Cool in pans 10 minutes; remove layers from pans, and cool completely on wire racks.

Split cake layers in half horizontally to make 4 layers. Spread Custard Cream Frosting between layers and on top and sides of cake; sprinkle with coconut. Yield: one 4-layer cake.

Custard Cream Frosting:

4 egg yolks
¼ cup plus 2 tablespoons sugar
⅛ teaspoon salt
1½ cups half-and-half, scalded
1½ teaspoons vanilla extract
1½ cups whipping cream, whipped
¼ cup plus 2 tablespoons sifted powdered sugar
3 cups flaked coconut

Combine egg yolks, ¼ cup plus 2 tablespoons sugar, and salt in top of a double boiler. Place over boiling water. Slowly add half-and-half, stirring with a wire whisk. Bring water to a boil; reduce heat to low. Cook, stirring constantly, until mixture coats a metal spoon. Re-move from heat; stir in vanilla. Chill thoroughly.

Fold whipped cream, powdered sugar, and coconut into custard. Yield: enough for one 4-layer cake.

PINEAPPLE PECAN CAKE

2 eggs
1½ cups sugar
¼ cup firmly packed brown sugar
2 cups all-purpose flour
2 teaspoons baking soda
1 (20-ounce) can crushed pineapple, undrained
1½ teaspoons vanilla extract
½ cup chopped pecans
Frosting (recipe follows)
1½ cups coarsely chopped pecans

Combine eggs in a medium mixing bowl; beat until thick and lemon colored at medium speed of an electric mixer. Gradually add sugar, beating until smooth. Add flour, soda, pine-apple, and vanilla; beat well. Stir in ½ cup chopped pecans.

Pour batter into a well-greased 13- x 9- x 2-inch glass baking dish. Bake at 325° for 40 minutes or until a wooden pick inserted in center comes out clean. Cool in baking dish 10 minutes; remove from dish, and cool completely. Spread frosting on top and sides of cake. Garnish top with 1½ cups coarsely chopped pecans. Cut into squares to serve. Yield: one 13- x 9-inch cake.

Frosting:

1 (8-ounce) package cream cheese, softened
¼ cup plus 2 tablespoons butter, softened
1 (16-ounce) package powdered sugar, sifted
1 teaspoon vanilla extract

Beat cream cheese and butter until light and fluffy; gradually add sugar and vanilla, beating well. Yield: enough for one 13- x 9-inch cake.

Electric lights for the tree came as early as 1906.

THE work of decorating the Christmas tree in the home is made light, bright, clean, and safe by the use of electricity, and the effect is far prettier than the old way by candles. Get an Edison Outfit and avoid trouble and danger. The outfit as shown comes in a box in sets of 8, 16, 24 or 32 lamps

The Historic New Orleans Collection, 533 Royal Street

POSADA DINNER

Los Pastores (The Shepherds), *mystery play of the 1700s, is still performed during the Christmas season in the Southwest.*

One of the loveliest of the Southern Christmas pageants takes place in the Southwest where the Mexican influence imbues devout Christian observances with beauty and color. Las Posadas (The Inns) is a symbolic reenactment of the arrival of Mary and Joseph in Bethlehem and their search for a place to stay. Costumed travelers sing at each house, asking admittance; from inside, singers refuse them. The guests are welcomed at last and after offering gifts to the Child, all go into the dining room where traditional Mexican fare is served.

GUACAMOLE WITH POMEGRANATE SEEDS
FRIED TORTILLA CHIPS
TURKEY MOLE
SWEET POTATO EMPANADAS

Serves 8

Fried Tortilla Chips are the right taste and texture to complement Turkey Mole, as in Olé!

GUACAMOLE WITH POMEGRANATE SEEDS

4 medium avocados, peeled and mashed
¼ cup plus ½ teaspoon lemon or lime juice
1 large onion, minced
3 small cloves garlic, crushed
2 medium tomatoes, peeled and finely chopped
1½ teaspoons olive oil
4 to 5 drops hot sauce (optional)
Lettuce leaves
Pomegranate seeds (optional)

Combine avocados, juice, onion, garlic, tomatoes, and oil in a large bowl; mix well. Stir in hot sauce, if desired. Cover and chill thoroughly. Serve on lettuce leaves. Sprinkle with pomegranate seeds, if desired. Serve with tortilla chips. Yield: about 3½ cups.

FRIED TORTILLA CHIPS

24 corn tortillas
Vegetable oil
Salt to taste

Cut each tortilla into four 2-inch squares. Heat oil to 390° in a Dutch oven. Fry tortillas, a few at a time, until crisp and golden brown, turning frequently. Drain. Sprinkle with salt to taste. Yield: 8 dozen.

TURKEY MOLE

1 medium-size green pepper, coarsely chopped
1 small onion, quartered
½ cup whole almonds
¼ cup raisins
3 cloves garlic
2 tablespoons shortening, melted
¼ cup cracker crumbs
2 tablespoons chili powder
1 teaspoon salt
½ teaspoon anise seeds
2 cups water
1 cup flour
1 (6-pound) turkey breast, cut into 8 pieces
Vegetable oil

Chop coarsley the green pepper, onion, almonds, raisins, and garlic. Or process in food processor 3 to 5 seconds; scrape sides and process an additional 3 to 5 seconds.

Sauté chopped mixture in shortening in a medium saucepan until lightly browned. Add cracker crumbs, chili powder, salt, anise seeds, and water; simmer 15 minutes. Set aside.

Place flour in a plastic or paper bag. Add 2 to 3 pieces of turkey to bag; shake well. Repeat with remaining turkey.

Heat 1 inch of oil in a large skillet to 350°; add turkey, and fry 20 minutes or until golden brown, turning occasionally.

Place skin side up in a 13- x 9-x 2-inch baking dish. Pour sautéed mixture over turkey. Add water to cover. Bake at 325° for 2 hours. Yield: 8 servings.

SWEET POTATO EMPANADAS

4 cups all-purpose flour
1 teaspoon salt
1 cup plus 2 tablespoons shortening
¾ cup cold beer
Sweet Potato Filling
½ cup sugar
2 teaspoons ground cinnamon

Combine flour and salt; cut in shortening until mixture resembles coarse meal. Stir in beer with a fork until well blended.

Roll dough to ⅛-inch thickness on a lightly floured surface. Cut dough into 5-inch circles. Place a rounded tablespoon of Sweet Potato Filling in center of each circle; moisten edges with water. Fold pastry in half, making sure edges are even. Using a fork dipped in flour, press edges of pastry together to seal.

Place empanadas on baking sheets. Bake at 400° for 15 minutes or until lightly browned. Combine sugar and cinnamon, and sprinkle over hot empanadas. Yield: about 2 dozen.

Sweet Potato Filling:

1 (16-ounce) can mashed sweet potatoes
½ cup pineapple preserves
¼ cup firmly packed brown sugar
¼ teaspoon ground cinnamon

Combine all ingredients, mixing well. Yield: 2 cups.

A CHRISTMAS TEA

It sometimes happens that time grows short, and we find ourselves in a small social crisis: Christmas is coming on at an alarming rate. No time now to issue invitations for an evening party; best answer is a charming tea to light up an otherwise dull afternoon. Holly and bright silver, a few holiday touches which are already in place, and it is only a matter of a session of baking.

Many bakers make their fruitcake for use the following year; the flavor deepens. Make it beautiful; we eat with our eyes!

Here, a Christmas tea in the dining room of the Judge Pringle home, Charleston, South Carolina, takes on special significance when the generations-old Waterford crystal tree is filled with red flowers and greenery to grace the table.

BENNE SEED WAFERS
BROWN SUGAR MERINGUES
HOLIDAY FRUITCAKE
CHARLESTON FRUIT TARTS

Serves 18 to 20

BENNE SEED WAFERS

¾ cup butter or margarine, softened
2 cups firmly packed brown sugar
1 egg, beaten
1 cup all-purpose flour
½ teaspoon baking powder
¼ teaspoon salt
2 (1.87-ounce) cans sesame seeds
1 teaspoon vanilla extract

Cream butter; gradually add sugar, beating well. Add egg; beat well. Sift together flour, baking powder, and salt; add to creamed mixture, beating well. Stir in sesame seeds and vanilla; mix well.

Drop dough by teaspoonfuls onto waxed paper-lined baking sheets. Bake at 325° for 10 minutes or until edges are lightly browned. Cool 5 minutes. Carefully remove to wire racks to cool completely. Yield: about 8 dozen.

Clockwise from front: Holiday Fruitcake, Benne Seed Wafers, Charleston Fruit Tarts, and Brown Sugar Meringues. Tea is a festive, easy kind of party.

Child's tea with dolls, 1900.

BROWN SUGAR MERINGUES

4 egg whites
1 tablespoon cornstarch
1 teaspoon vanilla extract
1 drop almond extract
2 cups firmly packed brown sugar
1 cup chopped pecans

Combine egg whites (at room temperature), cornstarch, and flavorings; beat until frothy. Gradually add sugar, 1 tablespoon at a time, beating until stiff peaks form. Fold in pecans.

Line baking sheets with waxed paper. Drop mixture by heaping tablespoonfuls onto waxed paper. Bake at 250° for 35 minutes. Cool away from drafts. To serve, gently remove from waxed paper. Yield: about 3 dozen.

HOLIDAY FRUITCAKE

4 cups raisins
1 (8-ounce) package candied red cherries, halved
2 (4-ounce) packages chopped candied citron
1 (4-ounce) package chopped candied lemon peel
1 (4-ounce) package chopped candied orange peel
1 (8-ounce) package chopped candied pineapple
6 cups chopped pecans
1 (8-ounce) package chopped dates
1 (8-ounce) package dried figs, chopped
4 cups all-purpose flour, divided
1½ cups butter or margarine, softened
1½ cups firmly packed brown sugar
6 eggs
½ teaspoon baking soda
½ teaspoon ground allspice
½ teaspoon ground cinnamon
½ teaspoon ground mace
½ teaspoon ground cloves
½ teaspoon ground nutmeg
½ cup brandy
Pecan halves (optional)
Candied cherries, halved (optional)
Additional brandy

Combine first 9 ingredients; dredge with 1 cup flour, stirring to coat well. Set aside.

Cream butter in large mixing bowl; gradually add sugar, beating until light and fluffy. Add eggs, one at a time, beating well after each addition.

Combine remaining flour, soda, and spices; add to creamed mixture alternately with brandy, beginning and ending with flour mixture. Stir in dredged fruit mixture.

Spoon batter evenly into two brown paper-lined and greased 9-inch spring form pans. Garnish top of each cake with pecan and candied cherry halves, if desired. Bake at 300° for 2½ hours or until wooden pick inserted in center comes out clean.

Cool cakes completely in pans. Remove from pans; wrap cakes in cheesecloth soaked in brandy. Cover with plastic wrap or waxed paper, and place in a tightly covered tin to soak for two weeks. Chill thoroughly; thinly slice to serve. Yield: two 9-inch fruitcakes.

CHARLESTON FRUIT TARTS

Tart pastry (recipe follows)
½ cup butter or margarine
1 cup sugar
2 eggs
1 cup chopped dates
1 cup finely chopped pecans
1 teaspoon vanilla extract
Powdered sugar (optional)

Roll tart pastry to ⅛-inch thickness on a lightly floured surface; cut into rounds with a 2-inch cookie cutter. Fit pastry rounds into miniature muffin pans. Set aside.

Cream butter; gradually add sugar, beating well. Add eggs, one at a time, beating well after each addition. Stir in dates, pecans, and vanilla.

Place 1 teaspoon filling into each tart pastry shell. Bake at 325° for 15 to 20 minutes. Remove tarts from pans while hot. Sprinkle with powdered sugar, if desired. Yield: 3 dozen.

Tart Pastry:

½ cup butter or margarine, softened
1 (3-ounce) package cream cheese, softened
1 cup all-purpose flour

Combine butter and cream cheese; beat well. Gradually add flour, stirring well. Shape dough into a ball; chill thoroughly. Yield: enough for 3 dozen miniature tarts.

YULETIDE SUPPER

Marion Harland aptly observed in the 1800s in *House and Home* that "we cannot divorce Cookery and Sentiment." So it is when Christmas brings the family together, sometimes the only real reunion of the year. The cook remembers everyone's taste in food and sees to it that each one is treated to his or her best-loved dishes. Family suppers, informal and full of catch-me-up conversation, are just as important as party-giving and party-going. And the food will be what has "always been served" at Christmas, although we have probably trimmed back a bit from the groaning board so prevalent among the Southern planter aristocracy. One such feast in South Carolina in 1839 called for five meats plus chicken and oysters and a wide variety of desserts and liqueurs.

Mrs. Harland would have liked Whiskey Kisses: ". . . The place of ardent spirits is in the medicine cabinet . . . But our eyes are not yet open to see death in wine-jelly or destruction in brandy-sauce."

CREAM OF PEA SOUP
or
CREAM OF CELERY SOUP
EASTERN SHORE SCALLOPED OYSTERS
CHICKEN SHORTCAKE
POINSETTIA SALAD
STUFFED CELERY ROLL
SCOTCH HERMITS
WHISKEY KISSES

Serves 6

CREAM OF PEA SOUP

1 (10-ounce) package frozen
   green peas
2 cups boiling water
2 cups whipping cream
1 tablespoon butter or
   margarine, melted
½ teaspoon salt
⅛ teaspoon pepper
Whipped cream

Combine peas and water in a medium saucepan; cover and cook 10 minutes or until peas are tender. Pour half of mixture into container of electric blender; process until smooth. Pour into a large bowl. Repeat procedure with remaining pea mixture.

Stir in whipping cream, butter, salt, and pepper. Cover and chill several hours. Serve with a dollop of whipped cream. Yield: about 5½ cups.

Note: Soup may be served warm with croutons, if desired.

CREAM OF CELERY SOUP

1 cup uncooked regular rice
2 stalks celery, thinly sliced
1 quart milk
1 cup chicken broth
1 teaspoon salt
¼ teaspoon pepper
Croutons (optional)
Green pepper rings (optional)

Combine rice, celery, and milk in a medium saucepan. Bring to a boil, stirring frequently. Cover. Reduce heat and simmer 5 minutes.

Gradually stir in chicken broth, salt, and pepper; continue to cook until thoroughly heated. Do not boil. Garnish with croutons or green pepper rings, if desired. Yield: 5½ cups.

Early Santa, laden with toys, decorates greeting card, c.1900.

EASTERN SHORE SCALLOPED OYSTERS

3 tablespoons butter or margarine, melted
2¼ teaspoons Worcestershire sauce
1½ tablespoons lemon juice
2 (12-ounce) containers fresh Select oysters, drained
1½ tablespoons minced fresh parsley
¾ cup breadcrumbs
3 tablespoons dry sherry

Combine butter, Worcestershire sauce, and lemon juice; mix well and set aside.

Layer half of oysters in a lightly greased 1½-quart baking dish. Spoon half of butter sauce over oysters; top with half of parsley and breadcrumbs. Repeat layers. Bake at 375° for 20 mintues or until hot and bubbly. Pour sherry over casserole, and serve immediately. Yield: 6 servings.

CHICKEN SHORTCAKE

1½ cups white cornmeal
¾ cup all-purpose flour
1 tablespoon plus 1 teaspoon baking powder
1 teaspoon salt
1¼ cups milk
2 eggs, beaten
¼ cup butter or margarine, melted
Creamed Chicken
Pimiento strips (optional)

Combine first 4 ingredients; mix well. Add milk and eggs; stir just until dry ingredients are moistened. Stir butter into batter. Pour into a well-greased 13- x 9- x 2-inch baking pan. Bake at 400° for 15 minutes or until lightly browned.

Cut cornbread into 4-inch squares; split squares, and spoon Creamed Chicken between and on top of each square. Garnish with pimiento, if desired. Yield: 6 servings.

Creamed Chicken:

¼ cup butter or margarine
¼ cup all-purpose flour
2 cups milk
2½ cups cooked chopped chicken
2 tablespoons chopped pimiento
¼ teaspoon paprika

Melt butter in a heavy saucepan over low heat; add flour, stirring until smooth. Cook 1 minute, stirring constantly. Gradually add milk; cook over medium heat, stirring constantly, until mixture is thickened and bubbly. Stir in chicken, pimiento, and paprika. Yield: about 4½ cups.

POINSETTIA SALAD

6 medium tomatoes
2 (3-ounce) packages cream cheese, softened
¼ teaspoon salt
⅛ teaspoon paprika
Martinique Dressing, divided
Lettuce leaves

With stem end up, cut each tomato into 8 wedges, cutting to, but not through, base of tomato. Spread wedges slightly apart to form shell.

Combine cream cheese, salt, paprika, and 2 tablespoons Martinique Dressing; mix well. To serve, spoon cream cheese mixture into shells; place salad on lettuce leaves. Serve with remaining Martinique Dressing. Yield: 6 servings.

Martinique Dressing:

½ cup olive oil
¼ cup vinegar
1 tablespoon finely chopped fresh parsley
1 tablespoon finely chopped green pepper
1 teaspoon salt
½ teaspoon pepper

Combine all ingredients; mix well. Yield: about 1 cup.

House hums with Christmas preparation in this detailed scene.

SCOTCH HERMITS

1 cup butter or margarine, softened
2 cups sugar
3 eggs
1 teaspoon baking soda
3 tablespoons milk
3 cups all-purpose flour
1 teaspoon cream of tartar
1 teaspoon ground cinnamon
½ teaspoon ground nutmeg
½ teaspoon ground cloves
1 cup chopped raisins

Cream butter; gradually add sugar, beating well. Add eggs, one at a time, beating well after each addition. Dissolve soda in milk; set aside.

Combine next 5 ingredients; add to creamed mixture alternately with milk mixture, beginning and ending with flour mixture. Stir in raisins.

Spread batter in a greased and waxed-paper lined 15- x 10- x 1-inch jellyroll pan. Bake at 350° for 35 minutes or until a wooden pick inserted in center comes out clean. Cool and cut into 2½- x 1-inch bars. Yield: 5 dozen.

Note: Leftover Scotch Hermits may be frozen for later use.

WHISKEY KISSES

1 cup vanilla wafer crumbs
¾ cup finely chopped pecans or walnuts
¾ cup plus 2 tablespoons sifted powdered sugar
1 tablespoon cocoa
¼ cup bourbon
Sifted powdered sugar

Combine first 4 ingredients; mix well. Stir in bourbon. Shape mixture into 1-inch balls, and roll each in powdered sugar. Store in an airtight container. Yield: about 2 dozen.

Chicken Shortcake front and center in this holiday supper. Poinsettia Salad and soup are also on menu.

STUFFED CELERY ROLL

1 bunch celery
3 tablespoons plus 1 teaspoon chopped pimiento
3 tablespoons commercial mustard-mayonnaise sauce
2 cups (8 ounces) shredded Cheddar cheese
1 cup finely chopped pecans

Separate celery into ribs. Wash thoroughly; pat dry, and cut into 10-inch pieces.

Combine remaining ingredients, mixing well. Chill. Alternating ends, press 2 celery ribs together, filled side inward. Add additional ribs one by one, continuing to press filled sides in and alternating ends. When completed, ribs will form a roll with cheese mixture in center. Wrap tightly in foil and chill. Unwrap roll; slice into ½-inch pieces. Yield: 1½ dozen.

THE MATADOR CHRISTMAS BALL

izzie Bundy Campbell joined her husband, Henry, on the Matador ranch at Ballard Springs, Texas, in 1879. Once Henry finished building Lizzie's "White House," she began to plan for their first Christmas ball, a party that was to become a memorable tradition for years to come. She invited all the neighbors, including the cowboys, and prepared a gloriously trimmed tree. The intrepid frontier woman cooked for days and produced an incredible feast against impossible odds. First, we'll need a wild turkey. From there on, today's version of the Matador Ball is a breeze complete with popcorn balls and doughnuts reminiscent of those that Lizzie served.

WILD TURKEY WITH CORNBREAD STUFFING
CORN PUDDING
SAGER'S OYSTER SALAD
BOURBON CHRISTMAS PIE
DEEP SOUTH SYLLABUB
DOUGHNUTS * POPCORN BALLS

Serves 12

WILD TURKEY WITH CORNBREAD DRESSING

1 (9-pound) young wild turkey
1½ teaspoons salt
1 teaspoon lemon pepper seasoning
12 cups cornbread crumbs
12 slices bread, cubed
4 cups chopped onion
4 cups chopped celery
4 teaspoons rubbed sage
2 teaspoons salt
1 teaspoon pepper
¼ cup bacon drippings, melted
6 eggs, beaten
About 1½ cups water
Vegetable oil
1 cup chicken broth
Apple wedges
Fresh sage sprigs
Fresh rosemary sprigs

Rinse turkey thoroughly with cold water; pat dry. Combine 1½ teaspoons salt and lemon pepper seasoning; sprinkle over surface and in cavity of turkey.

Combine cornbread crumbs and bread cubes in a large mixing bowl. Add onion, celery, sage, 2 teaspoons salt, pepper, bacon drippings, and eggs; mix well. Stir in water until desired consistency is reached.

Stuff dressing lightly into cav-ity of turkey; set remaining dressing aside. Close cavity of turkey with skewers. Tie ends of legs together with string. Lift wingtips up and over back, tucking under bird securely.

Brush entire bird with vegetable oil; place breast side up on a rack in a roasting pan. Bake at 325° for 1½ hours; cut cord holding drumstick ends together. Bake an additional 1 hour, basting frequently with chicken broth. Turkey is done when drumsticks are easy to move.

Spoon reserved dressing into a lightly greased 13- x 9- x 2-inch baking dish. Bake at 350° for 45 minutes.

Transfer turkey to serving platter, and spoon baked dressing around turkey on platter. Garnish with apple wedges and sprigs of fresh herbs. Yield: about 12 servings.

Cowboys enjoy the Matador Ball even without ladies, c.1900.

Southwest Collection, Texas Tech University

132

CORN PUDDING

½ cup butter or margarine
½ cup all-purpose flour
2 cups milk
2 teaspoons salt
1 teaspoon pepper
½ teaspoon paprika
6 eggs, separated
3 cups fresh corn scraped
  from cob

Melt butter in a heavy saucepan over low heat; add flour, stirring until smooth. Cook 1 minute, stirring constantly. Gradually add milk; cook over medium heat, stirring constantly, until mixture is thickened and bubbly. Stir in salt, pepper, and paprika.

Gradually stir about one-fourth of white sauce into egg yolks; add yolk mixture to remaining sauce, stirring constantly until thickened.

Combine sauce and corn in a medium mixing bowl; stir well. Beat egg whites (at room temperature) until stiff peaks form. Fold into corn mixture.

Gently pour mixture into a greased 2-quart casserole. Bake at 350° for 50 minutes or until center seems set. Serve immediately. Yield: 12 servings.

SAGER'S OYSTER SALAD

4 egg yolks
1 cup vinegar
2 tablespoons all-purpose flour
1 tablespoon butter or margarine
2 (12-ounce) containers fresh Select oysters, undrained
1 cup water
2 cups fine cracker crumbs
1 teaspoon pepper
1 teaspoon celery seeds
Lettuce leaves

Combine egg yolks, vinegar, flour, and butter in a medium saucepan; stir well. Cook over medium heat, stirring constantly, 10 minutes or until sauce is thickened. Cool completely. Chill.

For a Texas-style Christmas, Wild Turkey with Cornbread Dressing. Sager's Oyster Salad recipe is an interesting one. Save room for dessert!

Place oysters and water in a medium saucepan; cover and cook over medium heat 5 minutes. Drain and chop oysters.

Combine cracker crumbs, pepper, and celery seeds; mix well and add to chopped oysters. Stir slightly to coat oysters. Add half of chilled dressing to oyster mixture; toss gently until all ingredients are moistened. Spoon oysters onto a bed of lettuce, and pour remaining dressing over top. Yield: 12 servings.

Note: This dish can also be served as an hors d'oeuvre.

BOURBON CHRISTMAS PIE

½ gallon vanilla ice cream, softened
1 cup bourbon
¼ cup rum
1 cup dry mincemeat
2 baked 9-inch pastry shells
2 cups whipping cream
¼ cup sifted powdered sugar

Combine ice cream, bourbon, rum, and mincemeat; mix until smooth. Spread ice cream mixture evenly into pastry shells; cover and freeze overnight.

Beat whipping cream until foamy; gradually add powdered sugar, beating until soft peaks form. Spread whipped cream on pies. Serve immediately. Yield: two 9-inch pies.

DEEP SOUTH SYLLABUB

3 cups whipping cream
1½ cups sifted powdered
  sugar, divided
3 egg whites
¼ cup plus 2 tablespoons
  Madeira or other dry, sweet
  wine
6 oranges, peeled and
  sectioned
6 bananas, sliced
3 (8-ounce) cans pineapple
  chunks, drained
Grated orange rind

Beat whipping cream until
foamy; gradually add ¾ cup
sugar, beating until soft peaks
form. Set aside.

Beat egg whites (at room temperature) until foamy. Gradually
add remaining sugar, 1 tablespoon at a time, beating until
stiff peaks form. Add wine, beating well. Gently fold whipped
cream mixture into beaten egg
white mixture.

Combine fruit; mix well.
Spoon fruit in sherbet glasses;
top with whipped cream mixture. Sprinkle with orange rind
to garnish. Yield: 12 servings.

Note: This recipe for syllabub
is to be served as a dessert, not
as a beverage.

DOUGHNUTS

2 tablespoons butter or
  margarine, softened
½ cup sugar
2 eggs
2½ cups all-purpose flour
2 teaspoons baking powder
1 teaspoon ground cinnamon
⅓ cup buttermilk
Vegetable oil
Sifted powdered sugar

Cream butter; gradually add
½ cup sugar, beating well. Add
eggs, one at a time, beating well
after each addition.

Combine flour, baking powder, and cinnamon; add to
creamed mixture alternately
with buttermilk, beginning and
ending with flour mixture. Chill
dough 15 minutes.

Divide dough in half. Working
with 1 portion at a time, place
dough on a heavily floured surface; roll to ¼-inch thickness.
Cut dough with a floured
doughnut cutter.

Heat 2 to 3 inches of oil to
350°; drop in 3 to 4 doughnuts
at a time. Cook 1 minute or
until golden on one side; turn
and cook other side about 1
minute. Drain on paper towels.
Sprinkle with powdered sugar.
Yield: about 2 dozen.

*H.H. Campbell takes
a break with the
cowboys of the
Matador Ranch,
Texas, c.1900.*

POPCORN BALLS

1½ quarts freshly popped
  popcorn, salted
½ cup molasses
½ cup light corn syrup
2 teaspoons vinegar
1½ tablespoons butter or
  margarine

Spread popcorn evenly in a
lightly greased 15- x 10- x 1-inch
jellyroll pan; set aside.

Combine molasses, corn
syrup, and vinegar in a medium
saucepan; cook over low heat,
stirring occasionally, until mixture reaches soft crack stage
(270°). Remove from heat; stir
in butter.

Pour syrup over popcorn; stir
until all popcorn is coated. Let
mixture cool slightly; shape into
2½-inch balls. Yield: 1 dozen.

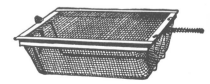

CHRISTMAS NIGHT EGGNOG PARTY

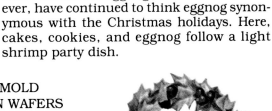

A party on Christmas night has a built-in festival atmosphere. Supper should be light . . . and late . . . to make up for all the excitement of the day; guests may be in the mood for winding down. Such a party quite readily includes eggnog. It is a peculiarly Southern mixture, very much like the German egg punch but ever so much richer. Some trace it to the English syllabub, but the latter contains no eggs and was used in the North at New Year's instead of eggnog. Southerners, however, have continued to think eggnog synonymous with the Christmas holidays. Here, cakes, cookies, and eggnog follow a light shrimp party dish.

SHRIMP MOLD
THIN LEMON WAFERS
CHRISTMAS CAKES
PECAN BARS
SALTED PECANS
SPICED ALMONDS
EGGNOG

Serves 24

SHRIMP MOLD

About 2½ quarts water
3½ pounds unpeeled medium shrimp, uncooked
1 cup butter or margarine, softened
¼ cup plus 2 tablespoons mayonnaise
2 teaspoons Worcestershire sauce
1 teaspoon lemon juice
¼ teaspoon ground mace
1 teaspoon salt
¼ teaspoon pepper

4 to 6 drops hot sauce
Paprika
Fresh parsley sprigs (optional)
Lemon slices (optional)
Pimiento strips (optional)

Bring water to a boil; add shrimp, and reduce heat. Simmer 3 to 5 minutes. Drain well. Peel and devein shrimp.

Grind shrimp or reduce almost to a paste in a food processor. Add butter; blend well. Stir in mayonnaise, Worcestershire sauce, lemon juice, mace, salt, pepper, and hot sauce.

Lightly oil a 4-cup fish mold, and line with plastic wrap. Pack shrimp mixture firmly into mold; chill several hours or overnight. Turn out onto a serving dish, and peel off plastic wrap. Sprinkle with paprika. Garnish with parsley, lemon slices, and pimiento, if desired. Serve with crackers. Yield: 4 cups.

Label on Santa Claus brand of shrimp makes the can look gift-wrapped.

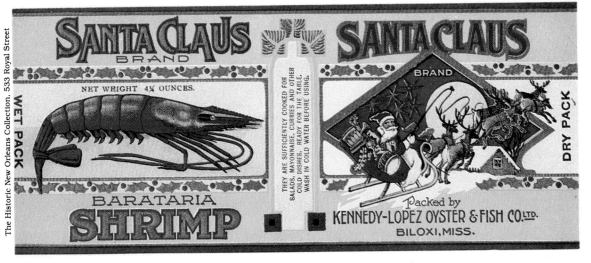

THIN LEMON WAFERS

½ cup butter or margarine,
  softened
¾ cup sugar
2 eggs
1 cup plus 2 tablespoons
  all-purpose flour
1½ teaspoons lemon extract

Cream butter; gradually add sugar, beating until light and fluffy. Add eggs, beating well. Add flour, mixing well. Stir in lemon extract.

Drop batter by level teaspoonfuls onto greased baking sheets. Bake at 350° for 8 minutes or until edges are lightly browned. Remove to wire racks to cool. Yield: about 5 dozen.

CHRISTMAS CAKES

½ cup butter or margarine,
  softened
1 cup sugar
3 eggs
2 cups all-purpose flour,
  divided
2 teaspoons baking powder
1 teaspoon ground allspice
1 teaspoon ground cinnamon
½ teaspoon ground cloves
½ cup milk
1 cup raisins, chopped
1 cup chopped pecans
Red and green candied
  cherries, halved (optional)

Cream butter; gradually add sugar, beating well. Add eggs, one at a time, beating well after each addition.

Combine 1¾ cups flour, baking powder, and spices; add to creamed mixture alternately with milk, beginning and ending with flour mixture.

Dredge raisins and pecans in remaining flour; stir into batter. Spoon batter into paper-lined miniature muffin pans, filling two-thirds full. Bake at 350° for 15 minutes or until a wooden pick inserted in center comes out clean. Cool in pans 10 minutes; remove to wire racks, and cool completely. Garnish with red and green cherries, if desired. Yield: about 3 dozen.

PECAN BARS

¼ cup butter
1 cup firmly packed brown
  sugar
1 egg
1 teaspoon vanilla extract
1 cup sifted cake flour
1 teaspoon baking powder
¼ teaspoon salt
½ cup chopped pecans

Cream butter; gradually add sugar, beating well. Add egg and vanilla; beat well.

Combine flour, baking powder, and salt; gradually add to creamed mixture, mixing well. Stir in pecans.

Spread batter in a greased and waxed paper-lined 8-inch square baking pan. Bake at 350° for 25 minutes. Cool and cut into 2½- x 1-inch bars. Yield: about 2 dozen.

Note: Recipe may easily be doubled and baked in two 8-inch pans.

SALTED PECANS

½ cup butter or margarine
1 teaspoon salt
2 cups pecan halves

Melt butter in a large skillet; add salt and stir well. Add enough pecans to form a single layer in skillet. Cook over low heat until pecans are lightly browned. Drain on paper towels. Repeat browning procedure with remaining pecans. Yield: 2 cups.

SPICED ALMONDS

1 cup sugar
½ teaspoon salt
1 teaspoon ground cinnamon
¼ teaspoon ground nutmeg
¼ teaspoon ground cloves
3 tablespoons water
2 cups whole roasted
  almonds

Combine all ingredients, except almonds, in a large saucepan; stir well. Bring mixture to a boil, stirring until sugar dissolves. Reduce heat to medium and cook, without stirring, until mixture reaches firm ball stage (242° to 248°). Remove from heat; stir in almonds. Continue to stir until almonds are completely coated and mixture hardens slightly.

Immediately pour mixture onto buttered waxed paper, spreading evenly. Cool thoroughly. To serve, break almonds apart. Yield: about 2 cups.

EGGNOG

12 eggs, separated
1 cup sugar
1 cup milk
1 cup bourbon
1 cup cognac
½ teaspoon salt
6 cups whipping cream,
  whipped
Ground nutmeg

Combine egg yolks, sugar, and milk, beating until thick and frothy. Gradually stir in bourbon and cognac. Chill several hours.

Combine egg whites (at room temperature) and salt, beating until stiff peaks form. Gently fold whites and whipped cream into egg yolk mixture. Chill at least 1 hour. Sprinkle with nutmeg before serving. Yield: about 30 servings.

With a gorgeous bowl of Eggnog, serve Thin Lemon Wafers and Christmas Cakes. Light meal starts with Shrimp Mold and Crackers.

ACKNOWLEDGMENTS

Ambrosia Cake by Mrs. John W. Green, Hattiesburg, Mississippi, first appeared in *Stallworth Roots and Recipes.*

Apple Lemonade courtesy of Mrs. Marie Spiess, Opelousas, Louisiana.

Berkeley Spiced Cider, Fig Pudding courtesy of Mrs. Jamieson, The Berkeley Plantation, Charles City County, Virginia.

Benne Seed Wafers, Charleston Fruit Tarts, Fruitcake courtesy of Thelma Mitchum, Charleston, South Carolina.

Bourbon Christmas Pie, Deep South Syllabub, Sager's Oyster Salad adapted from *Dining with the Cattle Barons* by Sarah Morgan. By permission of Sarah Morgan, Fort Worth, Texas.

Brittle Brown Sugar Cookies adapted from *Out of Kentucky Kitchens* by Marion Flexner, ©1949. By permission of Franklin Watts, Inc., New York.

Brown Sugar Meringues courtesy of Nancy Young, Charleston, South Carolina.

Brussels Sprouts with Dill Butter, Eastern Shore Scalloped Oysters, Maryland White Potato Pie adapted from *Maryland's Way* by Mrs. Lewis R. Andrews and Mrs. J. Reaney Kelly. By permission of The Hammond-Harwood House Association, Annapolis, Maryland.

Cheese Dates, Shrewsbury Cakes courtesy of The Mordecai House, Mordecai Historic Park, Raleigh, North Carolina.

Chocolate Cream Candy adapted from *The Jackson Cookbook* by Symphony League of Jackson, Mississippi, ©1971. By permission of Symphony League of Jackson.

Company Sweet Potatoes courtesy of The Smith House, Dahlonega, Georgia.

Cranberry Frappé, Sweet Potato Muffins adapted from *A Source of Much Pleasure,* edited by Virginia Phillips Holtz. By permission of the Mordecai Square Historical Society, Inc., Raleigh, North Carolina.

Danish Meatballs adapted from *Favorite Recipes of the Red River Valley,* collected by The Gleaners Class, First Methodist Church, Shreveport, Louisiana, ©1953. By permission of The Gleaners.

Easter Soup with Egg-Lemon Sauce, Greek Sweet Bread, Karethopeta, Pastichio, Rice Pilaf, courtesy of Mrs. Fannie Katzaras, Tarpon Springs, Florida.

Fresh Peach Ice Cream courtesy of Mrs. Clint Wyrick, Garland, Texas.

Georgia Catfish Stew, Ogeechee River Fried Fish courtesy of Joann Conaway, Springfield, Georgia.

Gingersnaps, Jam Cake courtesy of Mrs. Jan Thomas, Philadelphia, Mississippi.

Homemade Candy Easter Eggs adapted from *Virginia Cookery - Past and Present* by The Women's Auxiliary of Olivet Episcopal Church, Franconia, Virginia, ©1957. By permission of The Women's Auxiliary.

Huguenot Torte, Pineapple Pecan Cake, Syllabub courtesy of Nancy and Greg Allen, Middleton Place Restaurant, Middleton Place, Charleston, South Carolina.

Individual Pineapple Chiffon Pies from the personal files of Julie Benell.

Jo's Egg Casserole, Southern "Ice Cream" Grits courtesy of Jo Boone, Louisville, Kentucky.

Menu for "After the Race" prepared for photography by Chef Joe LeMunyon, Louisville, Kentucky.

Menu for "Mardi Gras in Mobile" courtesy of N.J. Stallworth, President, Prepared Food Products, Inc., Mobile, Alabama.

Menu for "Maryland Garden Pilgrimage Luncheon" courtesy of The Hammond-Harwood House Association, Annapolis, Maryland.

Menu for "Memphis Passover" courtesy of Mrs. Sam Steckol, Memphis, Tennessee.

Menu for "Moravian Easter Sunrise Breakfast" courtesy of Old Salem, Inc., Winston-Salem, North Carolina.

Menu for "Tree Trimmer's Dessert Party" photographed at Middleton Place Restaurant, Middleton Place, National Historic Landmark, Charleston, South Carolina.

Menu for "Wearin' of the Green in Texas" courtesy of the Dublin Chamber of Commerce, Dublin, Texas.

Menus for "Carnival Dessert Party" and "Rex Cocktail Party" prepared for photography by Marcelle Bienvenu, Chez Marcelle Restaurant, Lafayette, Louisiana.

Mississippi Cornbread courtesy of Mrs. Flora Thomas, Philadelphia, Mississippi.

Molded Potato Salad adapted from *Famous Kentucky Recipes*, compiled by Cabbage Patch Circle, ©1952. By permission of Cabbage Patch Circle, Louisville, Kentucky.

Neshoba County Fried Chicken courtesy of Gwen Alford, Philadelphia, Mississippi.

Old-Fashioned Tea Cakes courtesy of the family of Ruth Tittsworth Eakin, Shelbyville, Tennessee.

Pickled Shrimp, Sugared Nuts adapted from *The James River Plantation Cookbook*, published by The Williamsburg Publishing Company. By permission of The Williamsburg Publishing Company, Williamsburg, Virginia.

Pimiento Cheese Stuffed Celery adapted from *Flavor Favorites*, published by Baylor University Alumni Association. By permission of Baylor Alumni Association, Waco, Texas.

Pound Cake adapted from *Favorite Recipes from the Big House* by The N.G. Davis Family, Mobile, Alabama. By permission of Cookbook Publishers, Inc., Lenexa, Kansas.

Pumpkin Cake adapted from *Welcome Back to Pleasant Hill* by Elizabeth C. Kremer. By permission of Shakertown at Pleasant Hill, Harrodsburg, Kentucky.

Pumpkin Pecan Pie adapted from *Recipes From Old Virginia*, compiled by the Virginia Federation of Home Demonstration Clubs, Virginia, ©1946. By permission of Virginia Extension Homemakers Council, Austinville, Virginia.

Sautéed Walnuts, Shrub, Tiny Sweet Rolls, Wassail courtesy of Mrs. Mari Fehr, Summerville, South Carolina.

Savannah Baked Oysters adapted from *Savannah Sampler Cookbook* by Margaret Wayt DeBolt, ©1978. By permission of The Donning Company Publishers, Norfolk, Virginia.

Scotch Hermits adapted from *Aunt Hank's Rock House Kitchen*, compiled by Georgia Mae Smith. By permission of Crosby County Pioneer Memorial Museum, Crosbyton, Texas.

Shrimp Mold adapted from *Charleston Receipts* by the Junior League of Charleston, ©1950. By permission of the Junior League of Charleston, South Carolina.

Spiced Almonds courtesy of Mrs. Forrest Nestelroad, Clinton, Mississippi.

Strawberry Shortcake courtesy of Mrs. MacGreer, Mobile, Alabama.

Sweet and Sour Slaw adapted from *Prairie Harvest* by St. Peter's Episcopal Churchwomen, Tollville, Arkansas. By permission of St. Peter's Episcopal Churchwomen, Hazen, Arkansas.

Text material for "The Hunt" adapted from *Maryland's Way* by Mrs. Lewis R. Andrews and Mrs. J. Reaney Kelly. By permission of The Hammond-Harwood House Association, Annapolis, Maryland.

Western Kentucky-Style Barbecue Sauce courtesy of Elaine Corn, *Louisville Courier-Journal*, Louisville, Kentucky.

Brown Brothers

INDEX

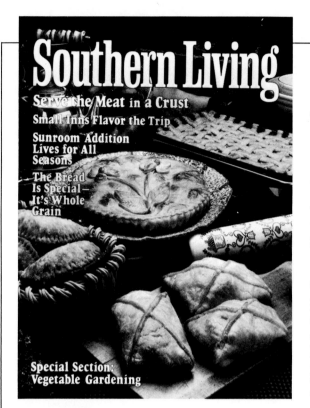